Alphabet Stories by Hermann Zapf

Es blühen auch im Schatten der Not viele schöne Blumen·

Alphabet Stories

A Chronicle
of Technical Developments
by Hermann Zapf

RIT · Cary Graphic Arts Press · Rochester/New York

Alphabet Stories · A Chronicle of Technical Developments by Hermann Zapf

The original edition of this book was published in 2007 under the title *Alphabetgeschichten · Eine Chronik technischer Entwicklungen von Hermann Zapf* by Mergenthaler Edition · Linotype GmbH, Bad Homburg / Germany, 2007.

This special edition is published and distributed by:

RIT Cary Graphic Arts Press, 90 Lomb Memorial Drive

Rochester / New York 14623-5604, USA.

ISBN : 978-1-933360-29-4

Printed in Germany

MY LIFE STORY begins in Nuremberg, where I was born on November 8, 1918, the last day of the German Empire. Those were turbulent days. On the day I was born, a workers' and soldiers' council took political control of the city. Munich and Berlin were rocked by revolution, and the Republic was declared in Berlin on November 9, 1918. The next day Kaiser Wilhelm II fled to Holland. The war ended.

To add to the chaos, the Spanish flu held Europe in its grip throughout 1918 and 1919. An estimated 20 million people died because of this epidemic, more than the total number of lives lost during the First World War by Germany and the Allies. Two of my siblings died of influenza in 1918. Famine hit Germany, reaching its peak in 1920. I was a very weak child, and in November of 1918 the physicians predicted that I had little chance of survival. In the following years, food shortages caused difficulties for everyone. In addition, the postwar period was overshadowed by political events in Germany. On June 28, 1919, the German delegation signed the peace treaty in Versailles. Not very much is remembered today about the consequences of the Treaty of Versailles on German life. It had tremendous economic and political effects, however, and finally led to the end of the German Republic on January 30, 1933.

San Francisco Examiner

An American Paper for the American People

Monarch of the Dailies

Reg. U.S. Pat. Off.

VOL. CIX MONDAY SAN FRANCISCO, NOVEMBER 11, 1918—SIXTEEN PAGES MONDAY CC NO. 134

"PEACE ON EARTH"

GERMANY SURRENDERS

(By Universal Service)

WASHINGTON, November 11.---The armistice terms have been signed by Germany, the State Department announced at 2:45 this morning.

»The peace conference started January 18, 1919, in Paris. The defeated states were not allowed to attend. On May 7, 1919, the terms for peace were presented to the

German delegation, but verbal discussions were not allowed. German officials strongly objected to the terms, but at the end they had to sign the treaty. Germany lost 13% of its territory with 7.3 million people, plus all colonies overseas. Parts of the Rhine provinces were to be occupied by Allied troops. Most of the merchant fleet was lost, and parts of the country's ore, coal, and grain supplies were confiscated.

The German people were angered by the inhuman reparations, and considered them to be unfairly punitive, for Germany alone was held responsible for the war. In the end, the Treaty of Versailles provided the best arguments for the rise of Hitler«. (From the encyclopedia: ›Der grosse Brockhaus‹ by F. A. Brockhaus, Wiesbaden 1953. Abridged).

The economic situation became more and more difficult. The devaluation of Germany's currency brought big problems to the daily life of most people, including my parents. Today it is incredible to realize that in November of 1923 one billion in paper marks was worth only one mark in gold. In the midst of all this turbulence, on January 11, 1923, the occupation of the Ruhr district by Belgian and French colonial troops provoked strong resistance from the German population. It is interesting to note that three weeks after the occupation of the Ruhr district, the National Socialists held their first convention in Munich. They rejected the Treaty of Versailles and declared it null and void. A coup in Munich on November 8 and 9 failed.

In the year 1925 my mother was relieved to send me to school, where I received a Quaker meal each day. This was a program organized by Herbert Hoover, who later became president of the United States of America. Because my weak physical condition was caused by malnutrition, I received a double portion, which made my brother very angry.

At home we didn't have many toys, but I could always play with those of my schoolmates. For instance, playing with the railroad trains of my friends was, for me, just like playing with my own toys. The reason they were willing to share their toys was because I let them copy my class exercises. This meant they could finish their schoolwork quickly and be free to play football. We were caught only once, when the teacher noticed half the class had the same mistake.

A few lines written by my brother Hans, who was four years older:

»Our childhood was spent in Nuremberg. Our parents lived in the Gartenstadt, a little neighborhood in the southern part of the city near the Ludwigs Canal. It was an ideal place for adventurous children.

The 1920s were not a good time for our mother. She was a great person who managed the household with very little money. As children, we admired her very much. Her life was not easy in those years, and she was busy from morning until night. As brothers, we stuck together. In contrast to myself, Hermann always had plans in his head, and was trying out his experiments in our home and in the neighborhood. Hermann installed all kinds of alarm systems in the house to warn us as soon as our parents came home. This was around 1930 when he developed complicated secret alphabet codes. His creations were hard to decipher, and it drove our mother crazy when she could not read all the messages.

I was the specialist in woodworking and I wanted to become a carpenter. But in 1928 I could not find an apprenticeship and finally I learned the brush-making trade, just to get off the street. As soon as I finished my apprenticeship, I was at once unemployed. My brother Hermann, when he was nearly 14 years old, became very interested in electricity. With great industriousness, he built a homemade electrical kit. It consisted of very primitive parts but was cleverly devised. It could all be stored in a shoebox. What a miracle it survived the destruction of our house during the war. For banana plugs and wire connections he found snap-fasteners and paper clips. In 1932 they cost less than ten pfennigs, but he had no money to buy them. Everything was made from discarded fragments and scraps. Fortunately

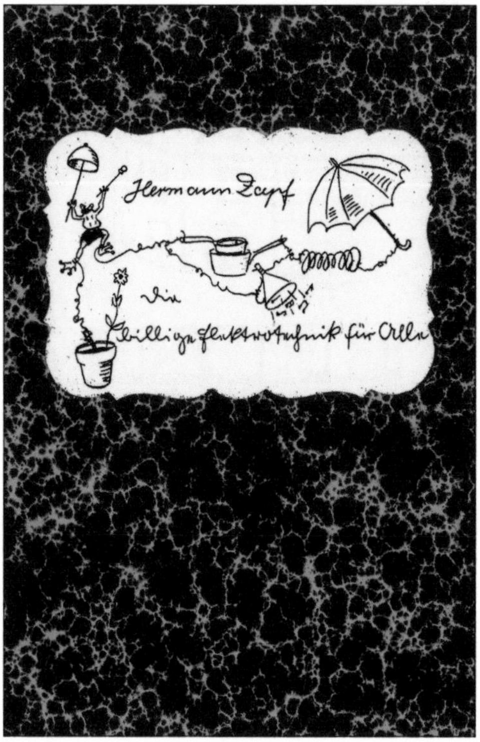

for him, he used only a Bertrix pocket lamp battery for his experiments. He understood how to use the power from his battery, but the use of high-voltage electricity was beyond his knowledge of physics. Yes, that was fortunate, I would say today. His crystal radio operated perfectly; every detail of it was also constructed with very simple parts. (See p. 96). We listened to Radio Munich on this homemade radio at night, under the bed blankets, and naturally our parents never knew anything about this. To ensure that we could do whatever we liked, he set up a warning system on the door handle with a double electric wire. Thank God it was low-voltage, because once our mother got a painful shock. It is easy to imagine what happened as a result of this slip-up. The installation had to removed that very night.

Hermann and a few friends wanted to establish amateur radio connections in our neighborhood. With diligence, he set to work learning Esperanto, an artificial international language which was very popular in the 1930s. He and his friends wanted to make radio contact with countries outside of Germany. But in 1933, the increasing political pressure and danger led to the decision to stop such plans, especially after his old friend Richard Fischer had to emigrate to Strasbourg.« (From: ›Hans Zapf: Mein Bruder Hermann, der Elektriker‹, essay in ›ABC-XYZapf: Fifty years in alphabet design‹. Wynkyn de Worde Society, London 1989. Abridged).

The overall situation in Germany was very depressing. To bring a definite settlement to the reparation payments for World War I, Germany accepted the Young Plan in June of 1929. This plan called for 34.5 billion reichsmarks to be paid to the Allied countries over a period of the next 59 years (until 1988).

Four months later the international situation changed dramatically. October 25, 1929, was ›Black Friday‹ at the New York Stock Exchange. This crash caused a worldwide economic crisis and massive unemployment. Germany's economic structure collapsed. In 1931, all our reparation payments were suspended, and from June to July of 1932 the Lausanne Conference reduced the German reparation debt to 3 billion reichsmarks.

In preparation for the Lausanne conference, the German government published a document which stated that 53,155 million reichsmarks (including the value of goods) had been already paid for reparations to former enemies.

And then came January 30, 1933: the dark day that brought so much disaster to Germany and the world, the day the National Socialists came to power. After the last democratic election to the Reichstag on March 5, 1933, all political opponents were eliminated.

Prior to 1933, my father had been greatly involved with the unions, so he had terrible trouble with the new government. On March 7th, my father was taken by the police, and a few days later uniformed men came in the middle of the night to search our house for weapons. The police claimed my father had confessed to having hidden weapons in our home. But my mother knew best what was in the house, and there were no rifles stored there. The only object they found and confiscated was a book by August Bebel, a founder and leader of the German Social Democratic movement before the First World War. We felt we were very lucky they did not find my Esperanto textbooks, and especially that they didn't find my little notebook from 1930 with the secret alphabets. Soon after this event my father came home from the Dachau camp. But for us children, these were very exciting days.

When I left school in the spring of 1933, my ambition was to become an electrical engineer. However, because of the new political conditions, I was not allowed to attend the Ohm-Polytechnical Institute in Nuremberg. It was not until 30 years later that I was able to fulfill my dreams – when I became involved with computer technology in the United States.

Not being able to study engineering meant I had to find an apprenticeship. Since I was good at drawing, my teachers – who were aware of our political problems – suggested that I should become a lithographer. Ten months passed before I found an apprenticeship in 1934. Every time I went for an interview, I was asked political questions. I was told that although they liked my work, they couldn't take me on. The last company in the telephone directory, Karl Ulrich & Company, didn't ask me any political questions. They also agreed my work was good, but at the end of the interview they told me they didn't do lithography, and therefore did not need an apprentice lithographer. Instead, they said I could become a retoucher, and could start the following Monday. I accepted right away and rushed home on my bike to consult the dictionary to find out what a retoucher was. And so I became a photo retoucher, starting my four-year apprenticeship in February of 1934. (See p. 101).

Retoucher

And now to letterforms, which determined the course of my life in the following decades. I have told about my path to calligraphy in a little story for an exhibition catalog for the city library in Nuremberg entitled ›Ein Gespräch eines Schülers mit Johann Neudörffer‹ (A pupil's conversation with Johann Neudörffer). It also includes my thanks to my teachers. Johann Neudörffer, the Elder (1497–1563) published a writing manual in 1549 with the title ›Conversation between two pupils‹. It is written as a dialogue between two young pupils with their teacher; and my story is written in the same manner. I first encountered the work of Johann Neudörffer in 1935 in the city library in Nuremberg. There I found his instruction books and examples of his virtuoso calligraphy.

»Dear Master: In 1935, when I was 17 years old, I became interested in calligraphy at an exhibition in memory of Rudolf Koch at the Norishalle Museum in Nuremberg. Koch was born in Nuremberg in 1876, and passed away on April 9, 1934. I bought his book ›Das Schreiben als Kunstfertigkeit‹ (Writing as an art), and a textbook about lettering by Edward Johnston, ›Writing and illuminating and lettering‹. Using these two books, I taught myself calligraphy at home using a broad-edged pen. I also studied historical examples that I found in the Nuremberg city library. Studying the work of the old masters from the sixteenth century affected me so much that I broke from the expressionistic style of Rudolf Koch and followed the teaching method of Edward Johnston. (See p. 98).

A few of my calligraphic studies from this time have survived the war, some pretty clumsy, for I didn't have a friendly teacher looking over my shoulder to correct my wrong pen hold and nib position. Dear Master, you would have suggested I put aside the steel pen and instead take up your quill. Of course, these steel pens are much too hard, they are probably made out of the best German Krupp steel, and surely not flexible enough to follow the swinging of the hand. But I've tried the laborious cutting which you described in complete detail, and the result was unsatisfactory. It looks so easy in your books. Perhaps you should have taken a look from your house in the Burgstrasse 16 across the street, to help me. In any case, I held the pen in the wrong position for two years, and my letters always looked so different compared to the forms in the instruction books by Rudolf Koch and Edward Johnston. Dear Master, what a pity you did not live in my time so you could correct my lettering exercises. When one tries to learn alone, the road is filled with many unnecessary detours. (From the exhibition catalog: ›Meister der Schrift – Hermann Zapf‹. Stadtbibliothek Nuremberg 2002. Abridged).

My boss at the firm Karl Ulrich & Company in Nuremberg very soon discovered my ability in lettering. From then on, I retouched letterforms. But during off-hours I also had to correct the work of my colleagues. Sometimes I could not get home until eight o'clock in the evening. My parents were angry, but of course they could not do anything about it. When it came time to take the journeyman's examination at the ›Handwerkskammer‹ in 1938, my father told me to refuse the request because I had been made to do too many other tasks during my four-year apprenticeship. This caused a lot of problems at a time when absolute obedience was paramount.

On the day I finished my apprenticeship, I handed in my resignation and a few days later, went to Frankfurt – without a journeyman's certificate in my pocket. I wouldn't have stood a chance of getting a work permit for another company in Nuremberg, since they could have checked everything in the so-called ›Arbeitsbuch‹ (labor book) which everyone had to have. In Frankfurt, I went to the ›Werkstatt Haus zum Fürsteneck‹, which was run by Paul Koch, son of Rudolf Koch. The Haus zum Fürsteneck was located in the historic part of Frankfurt, in the Fahrgasse opposite the cathedral. It was a castle-like building, erected in 1362, with four turrets and a big roof. This building was completely destroyed during the 1944 air raids on Frankfurt, along with almost every other structure in the historic section.

Paul Koch's specialty was the printing of musical notation in two colors. He cut music type himself in steel. (Paul Koch was born in 1906. Shortly before the end of World War II, he was captured in Poland by the Russians and never returned home.) The printing at the ›Haus zum Fürsteneck‹ was done on a handpress. My tasks in the workshop were mainly typography and the writing of song books.

It was a wonderful time for me even though I wasn't making much money. But from time to time I sent money to my parents in Nuremberg, concealing the reality of my financial situation. In Paul Koch's workshop I had the very best opportunities to learn the art of typography and to meet many local personalities. My only regret was that Fritz Kredel, whose work I admired immensely, had emigrated shortly before I came to Frankfurt, like several of his friends.

»During my time in Frankfurt, my best source of information about Rudolf Koch, Fritz Kredel and Berthold Wolpe was Paul Koch. He had known all of the artists connected to the ›Werkstatt‹, the workshop and studio of his father in Offenbach. In 1938, no one from the former group at Offenbach was there any longer, the political circumstances had pushed them away: Berthold Wolpe emigrated to London in 1935, and in 1936 Fritz Kredel went with his family to Austria and from there two years later to New York. Also in 1938, I arrived in Frankfurt. It was strange to me that the new people at Offenbach in 1938 were very reserved and did not speak much about Rudolf Koch and his friends who had worked with him. At first, I did not understand why. But I had conversations with Rudolf Koch's widow, Mrs. Rosa Koch, whose memory was still fresh at that time. She told me more about life in the 1920s and 1930s in Offenbach after the great inflation and depression in Germany. From her, I learned more details about the daily life and spirit of the Offenbach Werkstatt, and about the people who were part of it, especially Fritz Kredel and Berthold Wolpe (born in 1905 in Offenbach) who came to the Werkstatt in 1924. I also learned about Friedrich Heinrichsen, Karl Vollmer and Richard Bender.

Richard Bender's name also appears on the ›Deutschlandkarte‹, the great map of Germany, which was a project of Koch, Kredel, Wolpe and Bender. Through Paul Koch's printing office, the ›Haus zum Fürsteneck‹, I met Richard Bender – the last remaining member of Rudolf Koch's group in Frankfurt. I visited him in his studio in the spring of 1938 after my move from Nuremberg to Frankfurt. Bender was a very shy artist, who was still working in the studio room that the larger group had shared in the Städel Art Institute. The climate in Germany changed drastically after 1933. There were only a few real friends you could trust completely and know they would not inform the security police if you said something against the new political environment. Bender was very cautious and secretive about the studio room because it contained a potentially dangerous secret. One day he showed me a huge collection of historic arms stored in a heavy old closet; bayonets and other Hessian military items all belonging to Fritz Kredel. There were flintlock rifles with beautifully chiseled ornaments and other objects in perfect condition. Kredel's love for uniforms and military items probably stemmed from his father's professional military background. At the time of my visit to Bender's studio I was just 20 years old. Only later did I become aware of the level of trust and absolute discretion that has led Richard Bender to show me this unusual collection of Fritz Kredel's. In the political environment in Germany in the 1930s, the possession of any arms was extremely dangerous and even more so since they belonged to a person who had emigrated«. (From: Hermann Zapf ›The World of Fritz Kredel‹ in ›Fritz Kredel 1900–1973‹. Edited by Mathilde Kredel Brown and Judith Kredel Brown. The Arts of the Book Collection, Yale University, New Haven; The Grolier Club, New York; Odenwald Museum, Michelstadt/Germany 2000. Abridged).

Alkor

While I was at the Fürsteneck I designed two typefaces for musical notation. First came the ›Alkor Notenschrift‹ for the Bärenreiter Publishing Company in Kassel. It was a music type designed to be printed in two colors, for use on the Typograph typesetting machine. Although it was finished in October 1940, only a few test prints using this typeface had been made for F. H. Krauss in Schwarzenberg. Unfortunately everything was destroyed when the Bärenreiter printing plant was bombed in an air raid on March 9, 1945.

A similar destiny befell my ›Musica Notenschrift‹; a music typeface developed with an accompanying calligraphic roman type. It was designed

Musica

abcdefghijklmnopqrsſtuvwxyz
ABCDEFGHIJKLMNOPQRSTUVWXYZ

for the publisher Ludwig Voggenreiter, and in 1942 punches were made in the traditional method for music printing by the C. E. Röder firm in Leipzig. All the steel punches and most of the drawings were lost during the air raid over Leipzig on December 4, 1943. I made sketches between 1938 and 1941 for an unusual slanted music type, but this was never put into production. The idea was that if the notation was slanted the eye of a musician could perhaps glide more easily through the lines of a sheet of music. Take only a look at Beethoven's score of the Ninth Symphony in D minor. It may not be just the caprice of a designer.

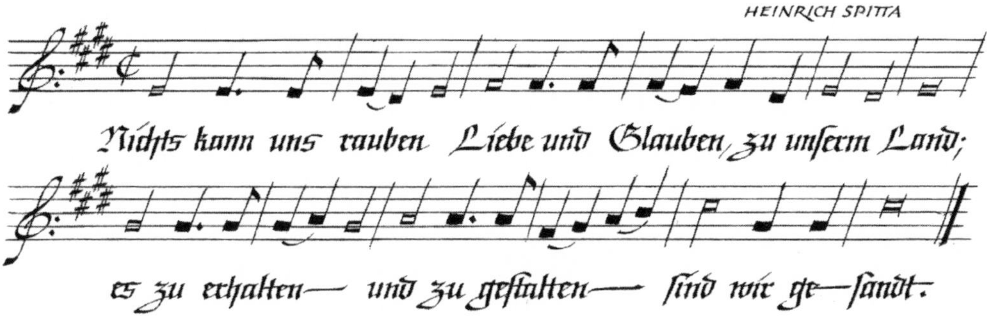

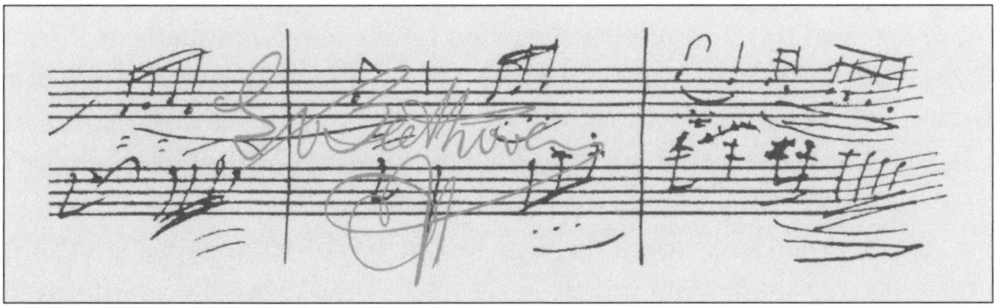

It was through the printing historian Gustav Mori that I first came into contact with the D. Stempel AG typefoundry and Linotype GmbH in Frankfurt. I designed my first published typeface for them in 1938, a Fraktur type called ›Gilgengart‹. The 36-point pilot size was hand-cut by the punchcutter August Rosenberger; it was finished in December of 1939. I received only 300 reichsmarks for the design of Gilgengart. When I appealed to the management of the typefoundry about this small payment some years later, they did not increase it and coolly responded: »We are the better businessmen«. The ban on Fraktur by the political rulers in January of 1941 was the end of any widespread use or popularity of the Gilgengart typeface.

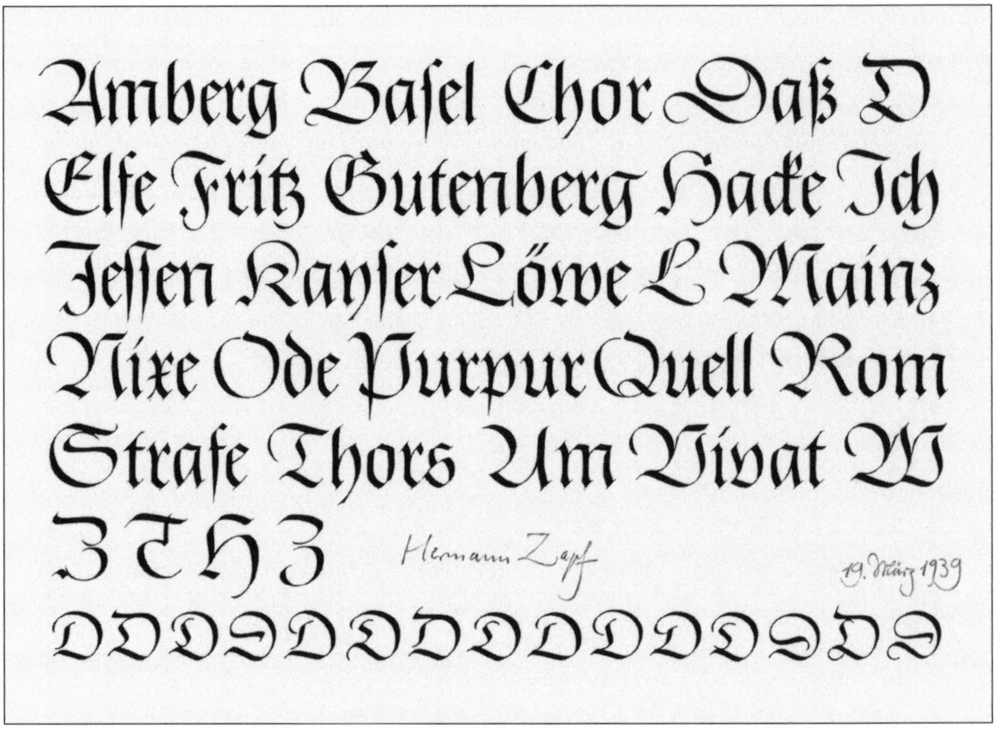

On April 1, 1939, I was conscripted by the ›Arbeitsdienst‹ (compulsory labor service) to reinforce the Siegfried Line against France near Pirmasens. I wasn't used to hard labor, my hand being skilled in the use of a brush rather than a heavy spade. After a few weeks I developed heart trouble and was sent to the office. There I wrote out the camp records and sports certificates in my best fraktur letters.

On September 1, 1939, the war began, which changed everything. Our entire Arbeitsdienst unit was taken into the army. I was informed that, unfortunately, due to my heart complaint I was not going to be transferred, but would instead be dismissed. It was not I who was sad about this, but my comrades who had to stay at the French border. However, in 1942, on April 1 – and not an April Fool's joke in sight – the Prussians summoned me to do my bit for the war effort. Not drafted to the air force, for which I had been selected, but instead to the heavy artillery in Weimar. That's just the way it is in the military.

I had problems with my superiors from day one. During training I often confused my left and my right, a problem which I still have today. To make matters worse, I was overly cautious and very clumsy with guns. I soon had the officers in a state of despair, bringing a premature end to my glorious career in the artillery. I was no longer welcome on the parade ground. I was first sent back to the office, and then to Jüterbog to train as a cartographer. From there we went to Dijon, and then on to Bordeaux to the staff of the German 1st Army.

In Bordeaux I drew secret maps of Spain, especially of the railway networks from Irun to the French border near Biarritz down to La Linea in southern Spain. The plan was to conquer Gibraltar from the land side by using heavy railway artillery. But Franco, that sly fox, mistrusted his ›friend‹ Adolfo (the way he addressed the Führer) and only used narrow gauge tracks to repair the railway bridges destroyed during the Spanish Civil War (1936–1939). Of course these tracks were of no use for the heavy railway artillery.

I was quite untouched in the cartography unit. But these backup units were forever being combed for young soldiers who could be commissioned. We called it ›Heldenklau‹ (pilfering heroes). Being only 25 years old, my turn eventually came. However, my commanding officer in the cartography unit was anxious to keep me, and sang the praises of my special skill in drawing maps of Spain. While the general was speaking, I took a fine brush and wrote out his rank and name in very small letters, without glasses or a magnifier. He took a close look at it, and his monocle fell off. Without a word of praise he continued on his way, and I remained the youngest cartographer in the German army. So you can see the fateful effects that letters one millimeter high can have.

Because of the work we were doing in the cartographic unit we knew a little more about the actual war situation, and secretly we wondered about the false news in the daily reports of our supreme command. But the surrender of the German 6th Army under General Paulus in Stalingrad in early February of 1943 signaled the war was already lost, with 90,000 German soldiers in Russian captivity. On the way to the camps more than 40,000 died of exhaustion. Only 6,000 prisoners of war held by the Russians returned to their homes, often years after the war ended.

During an air raid on Frankfurt in the early morning of January 29, 1944, the house in which I lived before I was called by the Army took a direct hit. I missed a connecting train south of Strasbourg on my way home from Bordeaux to Frankfurt. The delay saved my life because I would have arrived the evening before the air raid. I might not have been in the basement shelter so early in the morning, but being in the shelter would not have saved my life anyway; afterwards it was discovered that all eleven people in the basement were killed. I lost my books and some calligraphic items from my Fürsteneck days.

After this experience in Frankfurt I evacuated my calligraphic works and manuscripts from Nuremberg to Schwarzenberg in Saxony. They were stored in aluminum boxes in a vault at the F. E. Krauss works, along with the belongings of some other people. But after the factory was occupied by the Russian troops in the spring of 1945, everything was confiscated. Mr. Krauss was arrested and sent into the terrible prison in Bautzen. It was extremely difficult for the daughters of Mr. Krauss to talk to the Russian commander, and after several months only a portion of my property was returned. (See p. 102).

At the end of the war I was a prisoner in a French hospital. I was treated very well and could even keep my drawing equipment. The French had great respect for an ›artiste‹, as I think is still the case today in France. During my stay in the hospital, I designed a watercolor composition of a small bouquet of flowers, which was a symbolic representation of the circumstances in Germany. A broken branch and brown withered oak leaves represented the past and the destruction of the war. The bee was for diligence, and two little ants in the left corner showed an eagerness to work. The spring flowers stood for a new beginning after the war. The line underneath was a quotation from a former letter of F. E. Krauss: »Still in the shadow of misery many beautiful flowers are blooming«. (Shown at the frontispiece).

My health was not good at this time, but I had luck. Instead of sending me to the coal mines in Northern France, the French army released me in early June, four weeks after the Armistice. My brother Hans was captured in October of 1943 near Salerno in Southern Italy, and he returned home two years later from England.

The war ended on May 8, 1945. Here is the sad result of events from 1939 until 1945:

»The statement for Germany (the borders of 1937): 3,250,000 members of the military were killed; 300,000 civilians died in air raids; 1,550,000 people were missing from areas east of the Oder and Neisse Rivers; and 1,000,000 people in Russia, Poland, Romania, Yugoslavia, Hungary and Czechoslovakia died; in total 10% of the population lost their lives. The war cost approximately 657 billion reichsmarks. Of

16 million houses at the beginning of the war, 5 million were destroyed and 3.5 million were damaged. The Allied Forces attacked 131 cities and dropped 1.3 million bombs. The heap of ruins amounted to around 400 million tons. The homeless numbered 7.5 million. About 40% of the roadways, 20% of the production plants, and 50% of the schools were destroyed«. (From: ›Chronik des 20. Jahrhunderts‹. Harenberg Verlag, Dortmund 1983. Abridged).

In June of 1945 I went back to my parents in my home town of Nuremberg. The city had suffered terrible damage from an air raid on January 2, 1945. The unique old city of Nuremberg was almost completely destroyed. I was so closely connected to this ancient city before the war, especially in 1936 when I worked on various watercolor illustrations of the historic city in my manuscript interpretation of the poem ›Nuremberg‹ by Henry W. Longfellow (1807–1882). He visited the town 100 years earlier, in 1835.

It took a long time for life in Germany to return to somewhat normal existence. Everyone had to have the courage for a new beginning after the war. In May of 1946, Prof. Josef Käufer and Prof. Georg Trump offered me a teaching position to start again the lettering class at the ›Meisterschule für Deutschlands Buchdrucker‹ in Munich. But after a visit to the destroyed school building in the Pranckhstrasse on a rainy day, and seeing the black market atmosphere around the railroad station, I held it more advisable not to leave the hearth of my mother in Nuremberg for the time being and in spite of the critical food situation. Georg Trump was disappointed by my decision. But we became very close friends in the following years, and it remained so until he passed away on December 21, 1985, at the age of 89 years.

In the winter of 1946 I made my debut as a lettering teacher in Nuremberg. There were hardly any teachers in Nuremberg who were politically untainted. The lessons were part of a program aimed at re-establishing the trade unions in Nuremberg. We wrote our letterforms in an old school building under very primitive circumstances. The classroom had almost no glass in the windows, and some had merely been papered over. There was no heating; the exercises were done while wearing gloves with the wool of the right-hand fingers cut off to facilitate writing. We had to work by artificial light. The light bulbs had to be returned to the caretaker after the lesson. But everyone was very interested and excited about learning and preparing for a new start in a professional life after all the years lost for the war. Between 1948 and 1950 I gave classes in Offenbach at the same school where Rudolf Koch taught till 1934.

D. Stempel AG

In the year 1947 I went back to Frankfurt, where the Stempel typefoundry offered me a position as artistic head of their in-house printshop. I was not yet 30 years of age. They didn't ask for qualifications, journeyman's certificates, or references; all I had to do was show them my three sketch books done during the war, which contained my drawings and writings. A calligraphic quotation executed in 1944 in Bordeaux especially caught the attention of their punchcutter August Rosenberger. It was done with the finest Sommerville pen in red watercolor, the smallest letters only 1.5 millimeters high. The calligraphy is shown on page 21 in the original size. Here the translation of the German text I used at a time when I was still a bachelor:

»One may well hesitate before deciding whether to devote one's life to books or to women. Can you, when she has her whims, put a woman back into the bookcase? And what if a book, without asking your leave, were to go out of your library and onto another's bookshelf? Can a book demand that you read no other volume but devote yourself to its pages – despite your own wish to read another – or just as you are ready for bed (or intending simply to do nothing)? Will soups be over-salted by books? Can books pout or sulk or play the piano? Books, however, still have one blessed deficiency: they cannot kiss!« (Hans von Weber, 1872–1923).

Wie kann man bei der Wahl schwanken,
ob man sein Leben den Frauen oder den Büchern weihen soll!
Kann man eine Frau, wenn sie ihre Launen hat,
zuklappen und ins Regal stellen?
Wanderte schon einmal ein Buch, ohne dich zu fragen,
einfach aus deinem Zimmer weg in den Bücherschrank eines anderen?
Hat je ein Buch, stand dir gerade die Luft zu einem anderen,
wolltest du schlafen oder auch nichts tun,
von dir verlangt, du solltest gerade jetzt es lesen
und ihm allein dich widmen? Werden die Suppen von Büchern versalzen?
Können Bücher schmollen, Klavier spielen?
Einen Mangel freilich haben sie: sie können nicht küssen!
Hans von Weber

My first book at Stempel, printed by their house printing office was a monograph on the artistic work of William Morris. The idea for this book started back in 1938, during my time at Paul Koch's Werkstatt ›Haus zum Fürsteneck‹. The text accompanied me during my service in France and was finished shortly after the war. The monograph ›William Morris. Sein Leben und Werk in der Geschichte der Buch- und Schriftkunst‹ was published by Klaus Blanckertz in Lübeck in 1949. The frontispiece was cut in metal by August Rosenberger from my brush drawing. The book was printed in the Trajanus type designed by Warren Chappell. (Palatino Roman was at that time not yet available.) The Trajanus type, by the way, worked much better in conjunction with the dense prints from the Kelmscott Press books of William Morris. Here is the foreword from the book:

»The multitude of works ancient masters created within the time of their lives always presents itself also as a convincing proof of their diligence. The great variety of the ranges of art and science, which – to name some of the most characteristic representatives – a Goethe, an Albrecht Dürer, and a Leonardo da Vinci have filled with their genius, corroborates the truth of John Ruskin's words, saying that no law whatever has kept its universal validity to such a degree as the fact that the great artists were also great workers and that nothing was so astounding in them as the quantity of what they achieved during their lives.

We admire no less the creativeness of such eminent pioneers of art as Rudolf Koch and his great ideal William Morris, the English book-artist and artistic craftsman to whose memory this monograph is dedicated on the occasion of the 50th anniversary of his death (October 3rd, 1946). We in Germany however cannot think it our duty to go in for imitating his means of graphic expression. His work was unique in his own time in England, and so it has to be looked upon as closely connected with the problems of art and society of that time. But the German crafts of the book of today should go the way of working as honestly and devotedly as Morris did, in order to gain equal distinction.

This monograph is intended to make Germans more closely acquainted with William Morris the man, and with his longing and striving for the truth of art and for a more fortunate existence for mankind, ennobled and blessed by art – at the same time appreciating his eminent part in the recent German art of the book since the turn of the century, and pointing to the important suggestions Morris in turn received from the works of our German medieval printers.

Remembering all this, we may confess together with Rudolf Koch that William Morris belongs as much to us Germans as anyone born in our country; he drew his forces from our past and he will affect the future of our nation as one of the greatest men of our epoch.«

Novalis

Perhaps there was an additional reason for the Stempel typefoundry to entrust me with this important position of art director and to make me responsible for new designs. In July of 1946 I had sent them from Nuremberg very precise drawings in 36-point for a new alphabet, later called ›Novalis Roman‹. The drawings were production-ready, and the punchcutter August Rosenberger immediately got the order to cut the alphabet in 36-point. In October the first test prints were ready and everybody was hopeful that this new type would bring new life into the factory. (All three alphabets of Novalis are shown in ›Hermann Zapf and his design philosophy‹, Chicago 1987, page 21).

Novalis was a purely calligraphic design done with a broad-edged pen, accompanied by italic and bold versions. But the cutting was suspended because I perhaps too hastily showed another alphabet design to the typefoundry. This type was ›Palatino Roman‹, named after the Italian writing master of the sixteenth century in Rome, Giovanbattista

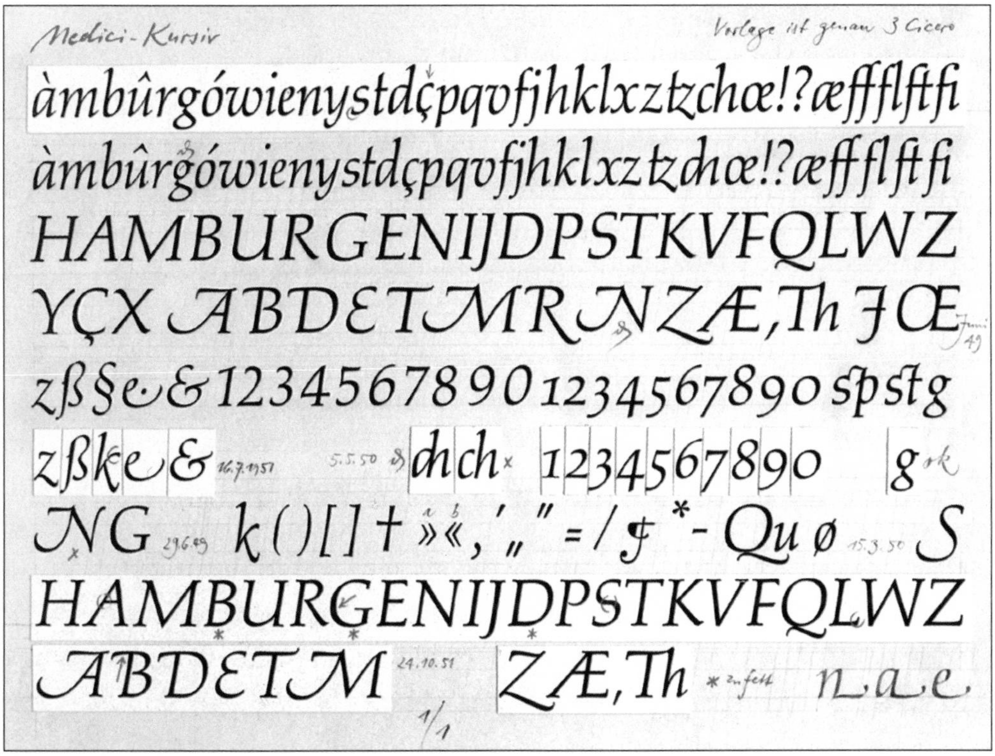

Palatino, a contemporary of Michelangelo and Claude Garamond. (I hope Palatino may one day forgive me in heaven and give me his blessing for using his good name for my typeface). The cutting of Palatino started right away in 1948; the Stempel typefoundry wanted to produce it as soon as possible in the hope that this classic type would become an international success – and it did. The type was produced later in 5-point through 72-point foundry type, with an italic and a bold, and also in matrices for the Linotype typesetting machine. Palatino does not deny its calligraphic background, as this is the source for all roman typefaces. The alphabet has its own unmistakable style; the design gives an impression of quiet restraint and strength with its graceful, clear shapes.

The very first showing of Palatino was in the deluxe edition on Japanese paper of the calligraphic collection ›Feder und Stichel. Alphabete und Schriftblätter in zeitgemäßer Darstellung. Geschrieben von Hermann Zapf. In Metall geschnitten von August Rosenberger, Frankfurt am Main‹. It contains 25 plates cut by the punchcutter August Rosenberger between 1939 and 1941, under very primitive conditions during air raids on Frankfurt. The text pages were printed in 1949 in 10-point Palatino at Stempel.

A second edition of ›Feder und Stichel‹ was printed in 500 copies for Gotthard de Beauclair's Trajanus Presse and published by the Insel Publishing House in Wiesbaden in 1952. At the same time, an American edition, titled ›Pen and Graver‹, was printed at the house printing office of the Stempel typefoundry in an edition of 2,000 copies on Fabriano mouldmade paper, published by Museum Books, Inc. in New York. The following text is from the preface written by Paul Standard:

»Calligraphy had long been dismissed as a mere handicraft. Yet this ›mereness‹ is no longer applicable even to handicrafts. In a generation's time handicrafts have won a respect surely comforting to the shades of certain Victorian pioneers. The late Eric Gill could not cease deploring the distinction made as between the fine arts and the applied arts. Surely a Leonardo or a Michelangelo, watching a wheelwright, an armorer, a scribe or a stonecutter at work, would see in each a fellow-artist who had mastered a special medium. Yet it has taken half a century to teach the layman to cherish and admire all artisanship and its component skills. Many now living still remember that when Edward Johnston (with William Morris and W. R. Lethaby) launched calligraphy's restoration to the living arts, it had first to fight down the mockery of the careless adjective ›arty-crafty‹. It was Johnston's influence in Germany, and later Rudolf Koch's example there that inspired most of our living scribes. The young author of PEN AND GRAVER has largely taught himself by the aid of the works of these two masters. Such was his passion for letters that he early sought a means of multiplying his original calligraphic sheets, to bring them

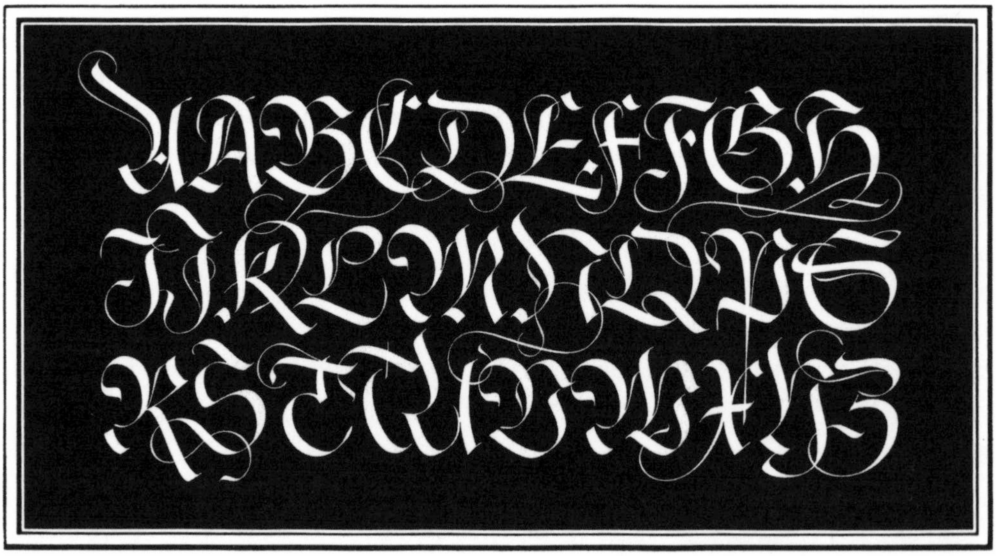

to a public far larger than could come to gallery exhibitions. Gifted and versatile in historic styles of letters, Hermann Zapf was fortunate to find in August Rosenberger the one man whose passion for them matched his own. Rosenberger, struck by the quality of the originals, decided to cut them, to print them carefully on Italian handmade paper, and so to provide enough copies to delight that larger public. For the reader's benefit the book contained half a dozen pages of German text in letterpress, chiefly to define the styles used in the twenty-five plates – each plate being printed in two to four impressions. The result was a volume titled FEDER UND STICHEL. The first edition, of 500 copies on Fabriano paper plus 80 copies on Japan paper, was printed in 1950 at Frankfurt in the printing-office of the Stempel typefoundry, which used the author's newly-cut Palatino type as a first showing for the texts. The book has been ranked among the finest calligraphic manuals known. It has won equal praise as an item of devoted bookmaking. For seldom has any book appeared with so many concealed evidences of simple affection and vigilant care for every part of its making. Jan Tschichold, a critic both stern and just, has told the present writer that no book produced in the past hundred years can show a comparable perfection of printing. Without sales organization, with no more than quiet merit to recommend it, FEDER UND STICHEL was destined for a swift American acceptance. Beginning in New York with the Typophiles, and the calligraphy students at The Cooper Union and at New York University, the news of its desirability soon travelled across the country. By the time Hermann Zapf could make his American debut at The Cooper Union Museum exhibition in October of 1951, the German edition of his book was well-nigh exhausted. His deepest satisfaction came from the knowledge that so many young students were triply cherishing his book – as treasure, tool and inspiration.

It should reach not only the workers engaged in the graphic arts, but also a wider circle of amateurs and calligraphiles. Indeed, it is upon the interest of this lay public that any growth in appreciation of letterforms depends. The existence of such a large and discriminating public, eager to welcome calligraphy and good printing, may well alter the entire outlook of American publishing, and so brighten the hope for a revival of the languishing art of printing.

To a layman it may seem strange to call calligraphy an agent for the improvement of printing, but such has been the historic mission of scribal work. The author hopes this book will help to bring to all calligraphiles a deepened response to all letterforms, and hence to other art forms as well. He thinks of our civilization as a unity of all arts, many proceeding from nature herself, many from man's response to nature, yet all bound together by some principle of interaction yet to be discovered and defined«. (Abridged).

The next big project with August Rosenberger was also developed during the war: ›Das Blumen-ABC von Hermann Zapf und August Rosenberger‹ (The Flower-ABC). This book had 26 brush drawings with a title page and a quotation by Goethe in calligraphy. Like the alphabets for ›Feder und Stichel‹, Rosenberger engraved the plates for the ›Blumen-ABC‹ during the evenings at his Frankfurt home, interrupted many times by air raids. His wife Klara told me that he never took any of his valuable books from the fourth floor to the shelter – just the plate on which he was then working. When the bombing ended, he got right back to work. What nerves this man must have had during these war-time conditions in the city of Frankfurt! Originally the ›Blumen-ABC‹ was to be executed for F. E. Krauss in Schwarzenberg, and Prof. Josef Käufer was to print the book in Munich. After the tragic incidents in Schwarzenberg at the end of the war, this was not possible. Then the idea was to print the ›Blumen-ABC‹ in a small edition for the D. Stempel AG typefoundry and the Heinrich Cobet Verlag in Frankfurt, enlarged with poems about flowers by Friedrich Schnack and Rudolf Hagelstange, using the Novalis typeface or Palatino. But in the end, it was done without the poems, and was printed by Otto Bickelhaupt at Stempel. We used paper left over from before the war, and we printed only 180 copies. A small part of the edition was colored by hand with special metallic paints for the various insects. The shiny effect was accomplished with a steel burnisher. The bloom of the wings of butterflies was done with pastels that had to be protected with fixative, for which special stencils had to be cut. No question, the ›Blumen-ABC‹ was an expensive production. (See p. 105).

A few bindings were done in full morocco by Gudrun von Hesse in Frankfurt and cost more than 200 marks each. This was a lot of money in the 1950s. Some of the plates of ›Feder und Stichel‹ and of the ›Blumen-ABC‹ are now stored in the ›Sammlung Hermann Zapf‹ (Hermann Zapf Collection) in the Herzog August Bibliothek in Wolfenbüttel/Germany. Unfortunately, the plate of the foxglove was lost during an exhibition in the Gutenberg Museum in Mainz.

These two publications were closely produced with August Rosenberger, who also cut all the pilot sizes of my typefaces for the D. Stempel AG typefoundry. Yet Rosenberger's name never appeared in any of their foundry's type specimens. I felt it was necessary to write and print an illustrated appreciation as a personal obligation to him. Here is an excerpt:

»AUGUST ROSENBERGER. The names of only a few punchcutters from the old days are known – for example, Johann Michael Fleischmann (1701–1768) who cut types for Joh. Enschedé en Zonen; and Edward Philip Prince (1846–1923), the punchcutter for William Morris and T. J. Cobden-Sanderson. The last great masters of our century were Charles Malin (1883–1957), who worked for Giovanni Mardersteig; Paul H. Rädisch (1891–1979), Jan van Krimpen's punchcutter at Enschedé in the Netherlands; and Louis Hoell (1860–1935) who cut Paul Renner's Futura for the Bauer typefoundry in Frankfurt, as well as the types for the famous Bremer Presse of Munich.

The art of cutting punches by hand for metal type now belongs to the past. Punchcutting was always a silent art – not at all noticed in the university art history curriculums. Punchcutters did not force themselves on the noisy art scene. They carried out their work with unusual patience in the serenity of their studios. They never wanted to be classified as artists. A little of the Middle Ages was still present in their craft, and they saw themselves as servants of typography. Who else so closely observes the details of a serif or the curve of a delicate bow? It is taken for granted like the everyday use of the alphabet.

August Rosenberger was my punchcutter, but he also cut many other typefaces, mainly for the D. Stempel AG typefoundry in Frankfurt, Germany, from 1927 until his retirement in 1962.

From the beginning of the war in 1939, August Rosenberger was as pessimistic as Dr. Wolf about its outcome (Dr. Rudolf Wolf had the position of art director at the Stempel typefoundry for many years, and was my predecessor). Despite their despair, they believed that the historic city of Frankfurt would never be bombed by an Allied air raid. Both men had already encountered many difficulties with the political party in Germany, in power since ›anno satani‹ 1933. The government was especially distrustful of August Rosenberger because of his Jewish-sounding name; they were also suspicious of the years he had spent in Russia as a punchcutter before he went to Stempel. In 1942, because of all the political pressure, Rudolf Wolf, our good friend at Stempel and a real gentleman, took a gun and shot himself to death. Among many other accomplishments, Dr. Wolf had designed the typeface ›Memphis‹, a very successful family of slab-serif alphabets issued by Stempel in 1929. Rosenberger had cut the punches for all the different versions.

Gustav Mori's type museum, known as ›Haus zum Alten Frosch‹ and located in the Falkengasse 3 next to St. Leonhard Church, was leveled in the air raid on March 22, 1944. It had opened only eight months earlier in July of 1943, in the very house occupied by the former Egenolff-Luther typefoundry with a big celebration. Nothing is left today.

The Stempel typefoundry suffered relatively little damage in comparison to the heavily bombed Bauer foundry (also in Frankfurt) and the Klingspor foundry in Offenbach. Nonetheless, the working conditions in Stempel's punchcutting department and printing office were very poor. It was not easy to get machines repaired or even to purchase the simplest materials needed for producing type. The heating did not work, and food continued to be rationed in those years after the war. It was a time when everyone had to hope daily for inspiration and contend with compromises. August Rosenberger and I earned extra money for living expenses by producing bookplates, postcards, and small prints. I made the designs and Rosenberger cut the plates.

August Rosenberger was one of the very last craftsmen in his profession to engrave in type metal. He was a man of unbelievable patience, and no job was too complicated for him. I never wanted to cut punches or engrave in metal once I saw the perfection of August Rosenberger's work. But I did want to learn firsthand a few more details about this craft and how much time is required to achieve such precision. An initial ›N‹ that I cut in type metal for myself was not very good in Rosenberger's eyes, but after hitting my thumb several times with the graver, I was filled with an immense respect for the engraver's art. In addition I learned patience and precision in the best possible manner. Punchcutting was much more than a craft; it was an artform with a centuries-old tradition.

While in my position as Stempel's art director from 1947 to 1956, the management of the firm did not permit me to mention August Rosenberger's name in a type specimen. If he had realized his importance and how well-known he was outside the company, he might one day have asked for a higher salary. Such is the poor attitude of business people. This publication, therefore, is an overdue tribute to the work of a man who was pushed aside throughout his career at the company where he had worked for so many years. On July 31, 1980, August Rosenberger laid aside his graver forever«. (From: ›August Rosenberger 1893–1980; A tribute to one of the great masters of punchcutting, an art now all but extinct‹ by Hermann Zapf. Melbert B. Cary, Jr. Graphic Arts Collection, Rochester Institute of Technology, 1996. Abridged).

After this excursion, we proceed to the story of ›Palatino‹, a type family developed over the years from 1948 through the mid-1950s. This type family was enlarged beyond the roman, to include an italic with swash characters, a bold version, and two titling alphabets, ›Michelangelo‹ and ›Sistina‹.

Aldus Book

A welcome addition to the Palatino family was ›Aldus Book‹, a version used on the Linotype system that was designed to be a little more narrow for book typography. It was the suggestion of Gotthard de Beauclair of the Insel Publishing House in Wiesbaden. Later, a version called ›Enge Linotype Aldus‹ was added and developed initially for the printing of the Rowohlt pocket books; it was condensed by five percent over ›Aldus Book‹. The Aldus alphabets are not based on types by the Venetian printer Aldus Manutius, who lived from 1449 to 1515. Originally Aldus was intended to be the light version of Palatino and later, for sales reasons, the name was changed to ›Linotype Aldus Roman‹. The proportions for the complete Palatino type family (stems to heights of characters) are: Michelangelo 1:12, Aldus Book 1:11, Palatino 1:9, Sistina 1:7 and for Palatino Bold 1:5.

All the kin of the Palatino type family are nicely described by Georg Kurt Schauer in the Palatino type specimen from the late 1950s:

»PALATINO: fatherly, weighty and stable, named after the great writing master of the sixteenth century, his presence determines the temperament of the Palatino types. Standing next to him with a lively spirit is PALATINO ITALIC. For the Linotype machine composition system, book sizes of an identical roman, mated with an italic and bold version, were manufactured. PALATINO BOLD, a robust member

MICHELANGELO ΦΕΙΛΕΑΣ

of the family, very useful when the need arises to support a title or add a special power. Charming, but a little imperious are the Small Caps for chapter openings. SWASH LETTERS are quite at home doing jobbing work, where their capricious expression is saluted. MICHELANGELO is very welcome at solemn occasions, these monumental capital letters express timeless validity. His stately sister SISTINA (p. 117) with her vigorous voice asserts herself in the noisy market of jobbing faces. PHIDIAS, the Greek cousin of the Michelangelo capitals, demonstrates the spiritual relationship between the Greek and Roman cultures. In addition, the HERAKLIT Greek can be used suitably with Palatino when a Greek emphasis is called for. An important branch of the family tree, LINOTYPE ALDUS Book and Italic will serve in book production when a more narrow typographic appearance is wanted. The most distant relatives are sometimes the most dependable. This far away relation is the muscle-packed brother-in-law KOMPAKT, for he handles the most complicated family problems with his left hand, without being clumsy or stern. The most lovely contrast is made by VIRTUOSA I & II, two sisters, but one has a more calm demeanor compared to the other. The Greek cousin of these Virtuosa sisters is called FREDERIKA, she has as much grace as her relatives. No company jubilee, no birthday, no other festivity should happen without SAPHIR, whose decorated forms are always an unusual surprise. Finally, GILGENGART will not be forgotten. She is a German descendant of fraktur alphabets but she looks so good standing beside some of the members of the Palatino family that we'd almost like to make her an honorary relative«. (From: ›Palatino. Eine weitverzweigte Familie mit der Sie immer zusammen arbeiten sollten‹. D. Stempel AG and Linotype GmbH 1953).

Melior Roman

Independent of the Palatino project, as early as 1948, I did legibility tests for a special newspaper face for the Linotype Company in Frankfurt. To achieve optimal readability in small type sizes, the idea was to facilitate an eye-guiding effect by designing shapes based on an oval fitting as closely as possible inside a rectangle. This became the design principle of ›Melior Roman‹. These shapes were not constructed with ruler and compass, but drawn freehand with my brush. Melior was issued in 1952.

In 1959 the Danish mathematician, inventor and poet Piet Hein developed a mathematical formula for such a special form and called it a ›superellipse‹. In the late 1950s, Piet Hein used his superellipse to design a traffic loop in Stockholm's rectangular city center, known as ›Sergels Torg‹. A reference to Piet Hein's superellipse is in my ›Linofilm Melior specimen‹ from 1966, which describes the redesign of metal type Melior for photocomposition. (See p. 115).

To make a script face is the most special challenge for a type designer. In 1948, experiments were made for a decorative script and later called ›Virtuosa‹. It took four years to cast it in all the variants. A Greek version

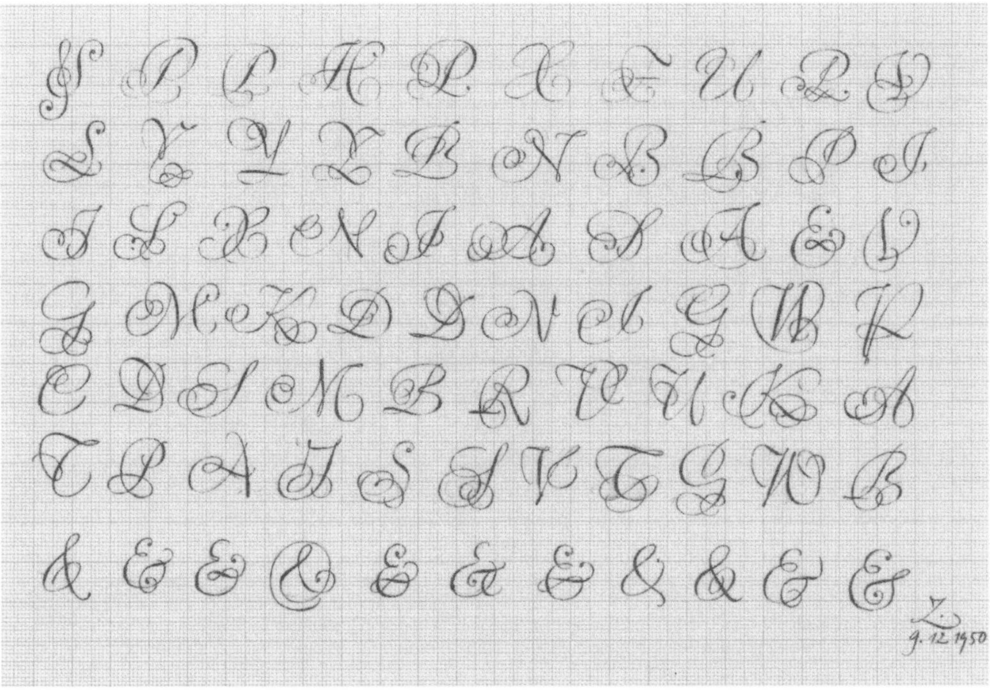

Virtuosa I & II

named ›Frederika‹ was added. Virtuosa was based on the letterforms in the Hans von Weber quotation from one of my sketchbooks done in 1944, during the war. (See p. 21). But because it was a metal type, Virtuosa was constrained by many technical limitations which had to be considered in the drawing of the different characters. We had no idea at all about the unlimited possibilities to happen 50 years later with the digital generation of letterforms. But for letterpress printing, Virtuosa was a special design and a successful typeface.

Optima Roman

In all these early years after the war, one of the most fascinating type projects was ›Optima Roman‹. It was my idea and I did not show anything to the typefoundry until the design was finished. I wanted to avoid any pressure by salespeople until I found the best solution by myself. Unfortunately, the sales manager of D. Stempel AG did decide the name of the type. My preference was ›Neu Antiqua‹, but this was rejected in favor of Optima. The history of Optima goes back to 1950. The type was released with only two variants – regular and bold, but also italic at the DRUPA printing exhibition in 1958. The unusual development process is told in the Optima type specimen from the D. Stempel AG typefoundry issued in the same year. (See p. 109).

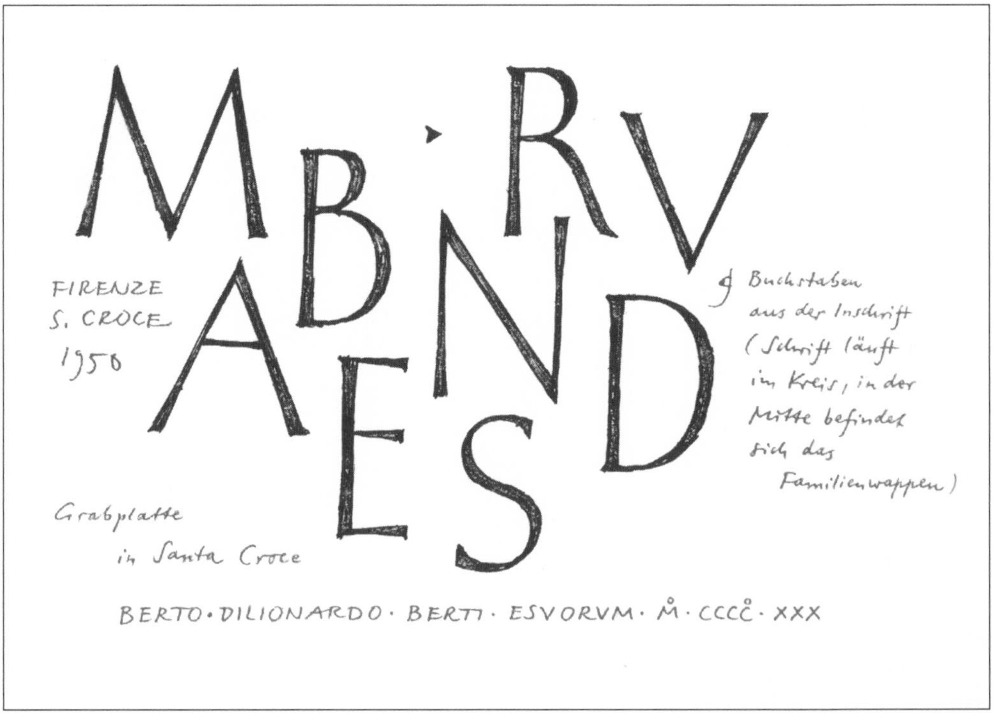

»OPTIMA. A new kind of type between a classical roman (Bodoni) and a sans serif (Grotesk): During a visit to Italy, I made studies of old inscriptions in Rome and Florence. My attention was caught especially by marble inscriptions on the floor of the Santa Croce Church in Florence. Every day, most people walked over these inscriptions so unmindfully. I got the inspiration one day to use these simple forms without serifs for a typeface. (See p. 107).

There are also very early Greek inscriptions without serifs. I was not satisfied by my first drawings, with thick and thin strokes based on the broad-edged pen at a 30° angle. I had to change the angle of the pen to get a vertical axis on the round characters. Optima Roman follows the proportions of the Golden Section in the relationship between the lower case and capitals«.
(From: ›Optima Antiqua‹. D. Stempel AG, Frankfurt am Main and Linotype GmbH 1958. Abridged. A digital redesign of ›Optima nova‹ and called ›Optima Titling‹ is shown on page 131).

In the year 1951 I married Gudrun von Hesse. She was trained as a bookbinder by Prof. Otto Dorfner in Weimar. It is curious that when learning calligraphy in Weimar, she used the same instruction books by Rudolf Koch and Edward Johnston as I did in Nuremberg.

In 1945 after the war ended, Gudrun could not return home to her parents in Potsdam because it was occupied by the Red Army. She went to Frankfurt and started her own bindery in 1946. At the time she was teaching lettering at the Städel Art School. An exhibition at this school in 1948 that included her work was the occasion of our first meeting. When I visited the show with Dr. Günther Lepold of the D. Stempel AG typefoundry there was a calligraphic piece with a text by Friedrich Hölderlin that caught our attention. This calligraphy was the origin of the ›Diotima‹ typeface in 1948.

It is an interesting connection that one of her ancestors was Johann Ehrenfried Luther (1700–1770), the very last of the typefounding dynasty Egenolff-Sabon-Berner-Luther in Frankfurt since 1533. The foundry was in the house ›Zum Alten Frosch‹ in which Gustav Mori established the Typefounders Museum in July of 1943. Benjamin Franklin, a friend of Johann Ehrenfried Luther, stayed there during his Frankfurt visit in 1768. To the regret of all, the beautiful building was destroyed in the air raid on March 22, 1944, along with the ›Haus zum Fürsteneck‹.

Our wedding was on August 18, 1951, in Wiesbaden. But the war in Korea (1950–1953) was not a very promising opening to a peaceful future. Our son Christian Ludwig was born in 1955. (He became a medical doctor. Considering the usual handwriting of physicians, they are obviously far removed from calligraphy).

On returning from our honeymoon in Italy I had to go to New York, because I suddenly received the American visa that I had been awaiting for several months. Paul Standard had arranged a big exhibition in the Cooper Union Museum – my first in the USA – together with works of Fritz Kredel.

In all these years of designing types, I worked on a book which was published in 1954 by the D. Stempel AG typefoundry in Frankfurt. It was ›Manuale Typographicum‹, a volume of 100 typographic pages in 16 languages, with quotations on type and printing. It was printed in oblong format by Heinrich Egenolf at the house printing office of D. Stempel AG. All pages were composed by Georg Tänzer. The Optima Roman type was not used in this book, as it wasn't yet available. The German edition was published by the Verlagsbuchhandlung Georg Kurt Schauer in Frankfurt, and the American edition by Museum Books, Inc. in New York City. This is from the preface:

»Typography is fundamentally two-dimensional architecture. The harmony of single proportions, the grouping of lines of type, the judging of contrast and balance, the symmetry and dynamic tension of axial arrangement – all these are the shaping tools, so employed by the typographer in a given task as to bring the reader a text in its most appealing form. The only limits to his fantasy are the suitability of his material and the traditions of historic style.

This manual seeks to show the myriad possibilities of the expressiveness and beauty of type, whether individually or in massed text, by the use of purely typographic means.

The letter's indwelling wealth of form is a fresh, unending astonishment. As there are many splendid types of earlier centuries that we still gladly use in printing, it may perhaps be asked why new types are designed. Our time, however, sets the designer other tasks than did the past. A new type must, along with beauty and legibility, be adapted to the technical requirements of today, when high-speed presses and rotary presses have replaced the handpress, and machine-made paper supplanted the handmade sheet.

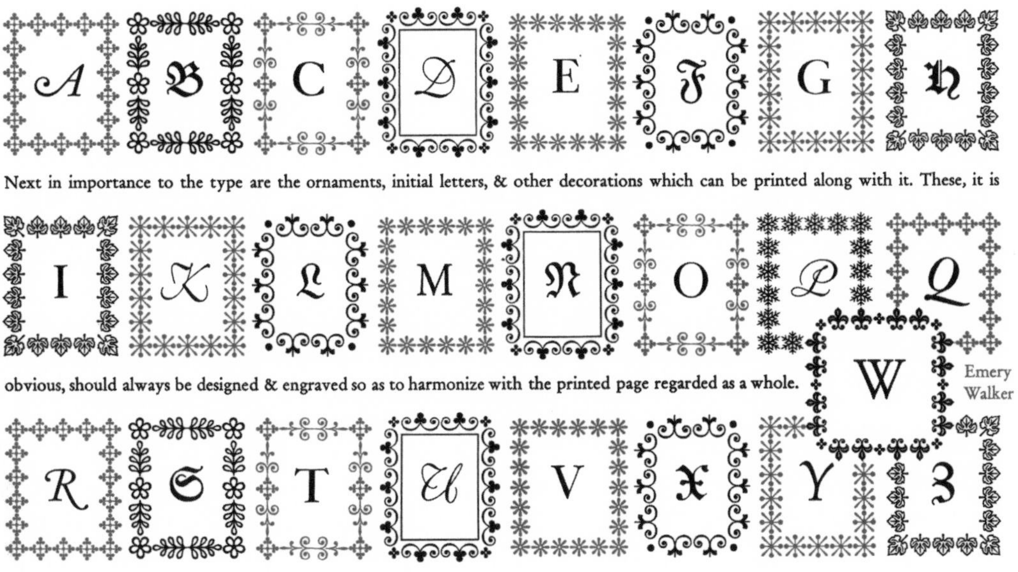
Next in importance to the type are the ornaments, initial letters, & other decorations which can be printed along with it. These, it is
obvious, should always be designed & engraved so as to harmonize with the printed page regarded as a whole.
Emery Walker

Just as musicians and artists seek to create some new expression of our time and link it to a rich past, so too must the work of type designers and typefounders remain bound to the great tradition of the alphabet«.

From ›Manuale Typographicum‹, here is an example of one of the quotations reflecting the importance of the alphabet.

»We use the letters of our alphabet every day with the utmost ease and unconcern, taking them almost as much for granted as the air we breathe. We do not realize that each of these letters is at our service today only as the result of a long and laboriously slow process of evolution in the age-old art of writing«. (From: ›The book. The story of printing and bookmaking‹. Douglas C. McMurtrie, Oxford University Press, New York – London – Toronto 1943).

A second volume of ›Manuale Typographicum‹ appeared in 1968 in 18 languages. This time it was in an upright format and printed with type faces from all over the world. (See p. 117). The main part was again composed by Hans G. Tänzer, my former apprentice at Stempel. He went to America in 1956, and worked at Joe Thuringer's Rochester Typographic Service, Inc. in Rochester/New York. With Hans G. Tänzer I could do the most eccentric and complicated typographic tricks. Unfortunately he died on November 20, 1991, only 62 years old.

In 1960 ›About Alphabets. Some marginal notes on type design‹ was published. A small book (11.3 x 17.7 centimeters), it was published in New York as one of the Typophiles Chap Books, with an epilog by Paul Bennett. He pressed me in 1959 to write about my life and my letterforms, during one of those bright Swedish nights in May on the terrace of the Foresta Hotel in Lidingö. Dr. Bror Zachrisson of the Grafiska Institutet in Stockholm had invited us both. Perhaps I agreed because I consumed too much Aquavit.

My text for a German edition titled ›Über Alphabete. Gedanken und Anmerkungen beim Entwerfen von Druckschriften‹ was translated into English for the Typophiles edition by my friend Paul Standard in New York. In 1970, a revised English edition was published by M.I.T. Press in Cambridge/Massachusetts.

›About Alphabets‹ was done as a typographic experiment by using only one type size (9-point Optima Roman) for the entire book. Differ-

About Alphabets

ent line distances separate the main text from the commentaries, which were composed with half the line spacing. The title page and headings were set in all caps. I have been told this little book had some effects over the years. One copy made its way to Israel and then to the hands of Jovica Veljović in Belgrade / Yugoslavia. After reading ›About Alphabets‹ he decided to give up his studies in painting at the academy in Belgrade and instead pursue his enthusiasm for letterforms. Today he is professor for ›Digitale Schriftgestaltung‹ at the ›Hochschule für Angewandte Wissenschaften‹ in Hamburg. Another copy of ›About Alphabets‹ went to Japan and guided Akira Kobayashi to Latin alphabets. During a seminar in Tokyo in 1982 I met Akira, a type designer, and again some years later in 1997 in Darmstadt. In 2001 he moved with his family to Germany, and became art director of Linotype GmbH in Bad Homburg.

Also in the ›About Alphabets‹ book is a report of my unusual meeting with the Arabian world:

»My first acquaintance with the Arab world came more by compulsion and accident than I wished or willed. As I laid in a Black Forest hospital with a Tunisian in May of 1945, out of boredom and as a useful pastime I learned from him not only Qur'an verses in Arabic but Arabic written characters as well. In early June of 1945 I was sent directly home from the hospital, but unfortunately fell into the hands of a French scouting party consisting of a Tunisian and a Moroccan, who took my discharge papers as a French prisoner of war, and without reading them set about shooting me.

An Arabic text, learned in my hospital days, saved my life at the last moment: ›One good man should not kill another good man‹. An exciting adventure for me; one I would rather not relate in greater detail«. (I suppose these words came out of my memory. This sura may have been from Chapter 9, Verse 5 of the Qur'an).

Al-ahram Arabic

Some years later I could used my Arabic lettering experiences when I received a commission to design a typeface for Stempel's agency in Teheran which was later called ›Al-ahram‹ (The Pyramids). It was mainly used by the biggest Arabic newspaper in Cairo, ›Al-ahram‹ a weekly founded in 1876 and one of the oldest newspapers in the world. (See p. 113).

»At the Stempel typefoundry in 1954, the need arose to cut a new Arabic type for export. This was no easy task, since in this type the customary kerned characters were to be avoided, to make the Arabic more useful for newspaper composition than the different fonts hitherto used. Along with one's own ideas which as a type designer one may often peruse for years in historical examples that are studied, rejected, reshaped and ever anew resumed, many interesting tasks arise from the special demands of a worldwide typefoundry such as D. Stempel AG.

يا ايها الكتاب سر الى سيدنا الاعز فسلم عليه بهذه الورقة
التى هى اول الكتاب وآخره يعنى اوله فى المشرق وآخره فى المغرب

I had occupied myself since 1945 in the study of Arabic letterforms (in the so-called Naskhi style), while within my calligraphic exercises I completed as my fiftieth manuscript ›Das Buch Suleika‹ from Goethe's ›West-östlicher Divan‹. (Three illustrations with polished gold and silver ink on Japanese purple paper from the Divan manuscript are shown in the Grolier catalog ›The fine art of lettering. The work of Hermann Zapf‹. New York 2000, pp. 21–23).

Prof. Joseph Hell of the Oriental Seminar at the University of Erlangen gave me the needed instruction and references. To be able to design a new type, I had to go deeper into the manner of writing the Arabic letterforms, and I busied myself for weeks on end with oriental calligraphy and with the extant Arabic printing types cut since the sixteenth century. Not every reader may know that Goethe too had occupied himself with Arabic signs in connection with the ›Divan‹, as appears in a letter to Christian Heinrich Schlosser, dated January 23, 1815: ›As to the Divan, little is lacking that I should learn Arabic, too; at least I shall so far practice the written characters as to be able to render the amulets, talismans, abraxas and seals in the original script. In no other language, perhaps, are spirit, word and script so organically fused together‹.

Naturally, I awaited in great excitement the judgment of Stempel's agency in Teheran, as at the end of 1954 my designs were dispatched for approval. My work found a very positive agreement, and my drawings needed virtually no changes. Work could now begin on the cutting. The first size of ›Al-ahram Arabic‹ was ready at the beginning of 1956, and a shadowed font followed a year later. Arabic alphabets are still used today in lands reaching from North Africa into India«.

My first teaching experience in the United States of America in calligraphy and book design took place in Pittsburgh/Pennsylvania in 1960.

Thirty years later, a participant named Ann Irene Walczak Hawkins remembered my start at Carnegie Institute of Technology:

»I was a member of the first class Hermann Zapf taught in America, in the fall of 1960. I'm sure we were the most under-qualified students he has ever had. The biggest problem was that we had no experience with a broad pen. This was a period when calligraphy, or even the drawing of alphabets, was not standard art school fare. But there was more to it than that.

With few exceptions, my classmates were like me: minimally educated in high school, no second language, no particular skills and terribly provincial. I had grown up in Pittsburgh and knew little of the world beyond. We were typical art students. We dressed in paint-spattered jeans. The girls wore black tights instead of stockings. Smoking was cool. We stayed up all night working on projects until we developed blue circles under our eyes that proved we were dedicated to art.

The idea of inviting Mr. Zapf to Pittsburgh was Jack Stauffacher's. He was our new typography teacher. The Dean of the College of Fine Arts, Prof. Norman L. Rice, gave his full support. Howard Worner agreed to suspend his design course to make time for the seminar. I've always felt grateful to the faculty who set this seminar up, but never gave a thought to who paid for it.

Meanwhile, Zapf was at home in Germany preparing an ambitious syllabus. He had been told he would be teaching a ›limited number of qualified applicants‹. I wonder if he would have come, had he know what novices we were. Lucky for us, he had no idea until he got here. We, in turn, also had a false idea of what our visitor would be like. It was based on Hollywood stereotypes of German commanding officers. So everyone was in for a surprise.

Carnegie Institute of Technology was founded by Andrew Carnegie who built libraries all over the world, ›Free to the people‹. His fortune came from the steel mills that made Pittsburgh the ›Smoky City‹. After the War, smoke control cleared the air but the carbon residue remained imbedded in the fabric of the city. Now the school is called Carnegie-Mellon University, or CMU. Back then, we simply called it ›Tech‹. The original architecture reflects an Industrial Age idealism. Hamerschlag Hall, housing the School of Engineering, was the flagship of the campus, crowned by a lantern-shaped chimney, a ›lamp-of-learning‹, emitting an eternal wisp of smoke.

The school buildings are strong and solid. Our class met in Baker Hall. The classroom was an old-fashioned one with real plaster walls, heavy oak woodwork and slate blackboards. Seating was at long tables, arranged one behind the other. We sat there waiting, that first morning, cleaner than usual, curious, excited and a little nervous. Stauffacher and Worner entered the room with a stranger but it took us awhile to realize that he was Mr. Zapf because he was so different from what we had imagined.

He had a very mild expression and manner. His thin brown hair was combed straight back from a high forehead and he wore a conservative suit and tie. The jacket came off, revealing an extra-white shirt with cuff links. The tie stayed. We were used to teachers dressing pretty much as we did and here comes this European, who had a very different style. Over the next six weeks, we got to know him more intimately than any of our other teachers, I think, because he made no secret of how he lived and worked. He knew and liked poetry, quoted philosophers, and was interested in science and engineering. It was orderly and on his desk, there was a single rose. It seemed he could write the history of the alphabet from memory. For his up-to-date types, Palatino, Melior and Optima, he had drawn inspiration from ancient inscriptions. He was enthusiastic about modern technology and its potential – and what might be done with these new computers. Carnegie Tech had installed its first computer just a couple of years earlier.

In Zapf's class, we constructed letterforms in a very deliberate way. The object was to develop some ability to indicate typefaces when making typographic layouts. He'd come around and use your pen to show how he would manipulate it to form the serifs. Taking it back, warm from his hand, you'd try to do what he had done. You couldn't do it so well, but got the idea that you can use the pen to make the shape you want, rather than just accept what it does automatically.

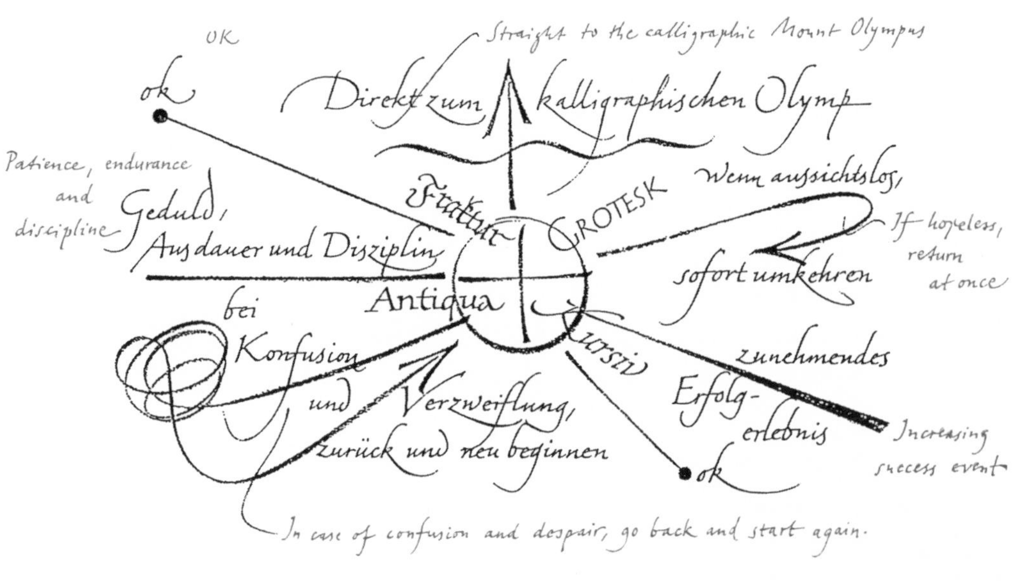

It was a warm and brilliant autumn. The leaves outside the classroom were cadmium yellow. ›I think this is such a beautiful afternoon‹, Zapf announced one day, ›I think we should go outside for our discussion‹. This was so unusual, that we had to have the special permission of the dean. I think we got his blessing. Zapf's plan was that we should work with ink in the morning while we were fresh and in pencil in the afternoon. This seemed odd. We were used to working around the clock. Hermann Zapf had other radical ideas. At home, he told us, he did his designing in the morning and spent the afternoons reading and attending to his correspondence. To us, the idea of an artist leading such a regular life was new.

We students didn't know about meetings around this time, arranged by Jack Stauffacher with Victor Hammer in Lexington/Kentucky, and other people, which led to Zapf's being commissioned to design a typeface exclusively for the Hunt Library being built on the campus and for Jack Stauffacher's ›New Laboratory Press‹. The building and the famous Hunt Botanical Collection were a gift from Mr. and Mrs. Roy Arthur Hunt, the Alcoa Aluminum heirs. As a young woman, Rachel McMasters Miller Hunt (1882–1963) had learned bookbinding from a pupil of Cobden-Sanderson. She achieved a high degree of accomplishment and developed an appreciation for fine printing.

It was a Cobden-Sanderson quotation, written in a formal italic by Hermann Zapf, engraved and printed on Japanese paper, that he gave each of us on the final day of the seminar. Framed on my wall, it reads: ›The whole duty of typography, as of calligraphy, is to communicate to the imagination, without loss by the way, the thought or image intended to be communicated by the author‹. This encapsulated the designer's role in the society«. (From: ›At Carnegie Tech in Pittsburgh‹, essay by Ann Hawkins in ›ABC-XYZapf: Fifty years in alphabet design‹. Wynkyn de Worde Society, London 1989. Abridged. See p. 95).

Book design

After giving up my position as an art director of the D. Stempel AG typefoundry at the end of 1956, my work as a graphic designer primarily involved book design for a few publishing houses. I worked for Suhrkamp, S. Fischer, Insel Verlag in Frankfurt, Büchergilde Gutenberg, Hanser in Munich, Phillip von Zabern in Mainz, Reichert in Wiesbaden, Hermann Emig in Amorbach, and others. I did not work for advertising agencies because their working methods were too hectic for me.

But everyone knows that as a freelance designer, you always have periods without any commissions. I had very few orders for purely calligraphic works, though sometimes I did publisher devices or logo designs. I welcomed commissions and opportunities to use imagination.

I received the biggest calligraphy job of my professional life in 1960 from the Pierpont Morgan Library in New York. It was the writing out of ›The Preamble of the Charter of the United Nations‹ in four languages, including Russian. A big reproduction was made of this by Ed Rondthaler and exhibited in the window of Photo-Lettering, Inc. on 45th Street in New York City. This was very close to the United Nations headquarters during the time of the visit of Fidel Castro and Nikita Krushchev. But they did not give a glance at my art since Nikita was perhaps too busy to even repair his shoes after his well-known appearance at the assembly of the United Nations.

Any free time I had was used to do work for myself, working without any pressure of deadlines, just for my own enjoyment. It is a fact, that to live purely from calligraphy is impossible in our time. But sometimes the weeks without any jobs can have a positive side, especially if you want to try something new. Towards the end of the 1960s I spent a lot of time doing calligraphic experiments with a new sgraffito technique. I prepared panels by first priming them with white color, then painting over with black oil color or casein, and, after this, scratching out letters in the half-dry ground. Several such big panels were executed with this sgraffito technique, and they have since been reproduced in catalogs and books. During this time, I also experimented with making three-dimensional letters in aluminum, cutting letters in plexiglass, and also engraving letters in glass with a diamond.

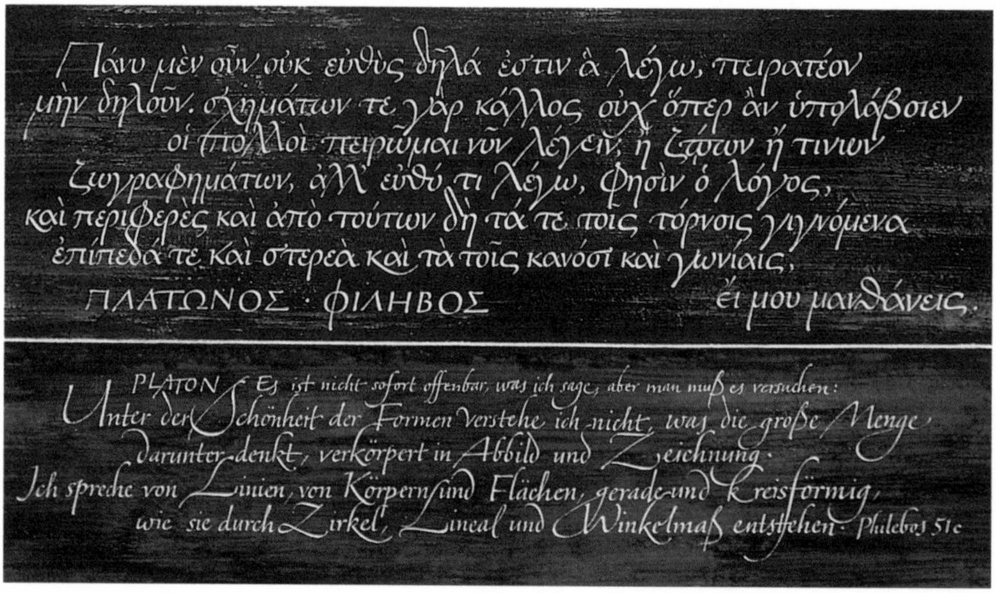

Hallmark Textura

What I learned from this play and experimentation with letterforms had an effect on my ideas for typefaces designed for photocomposition, such as the calligraphic alphabets ›Venture‹ and ›Noris Script‹ designed for Mergenthaler Linotype in Brooklyn, and especially those done for Hallmark Cards, Inc. in Kansas City/Missouri. In the 1960s and '70s, a close cooperation was developed with this firm, and I designed several typefaces exclusively for them. ›Hallmark Uncial‹ was done in 1969, ›Hallmark Textura‹ in 1969, ›Hallmark Scriptura‹ in 1972, and there were several more. The ›Hallmark lettering instruction manual‹ was an extensive work, and it is a great pity that it was used only in-house and never published for everybody to use.

Hallmark Film

In 1967–1968, Hallmark made the film ›The Art of Hermann Zapf‹. I still think back to this big event with great pleasure, remembering my involvement in the movie business. Hallmark's idea was to make an educational film that could be lent to art schools and television stations. It was an interesting project, but at the beginning it was very difficult. I was not familiar with the Hollywood language the movie people used, so I had to learn that first.

Our cameraman, Frank Robinson, came from Hawaii. He was used to big outdoor scenes with professional models. He demonstrated his ideas with sweeping gestures, and spoke in his Polynesian accent about shooting and takes in connection with story boards, stills he wanted to include, etc. My God, very quickly I realized we had absolutely different conceptions about the film. I wanted no outdoor scenes at all, no expensive movie stars. I only wanted to show single letters, my paw manipulating a broad-edged pen, and close-ups to explain the movement of the pen in making letterforms. In addition, I wanted special close-ups to be shot through a glass on which I would write. If we turned the film during production, it would look as though I was writing on air. At once my friends at Hallmark had a new term for this: ›frog views‹. How could I explain my thoughts to a wild man from the film business? But the frog view idea persuaded him and suddenly he said: »Great, Hermann, let's start tomorrow«.

I would like to add just one more detail about the making of the film. After long discussions and the help of a lot of alcohol, we started filming late at night. I was sitting at a slanted glass table with a hot spotlight in my neck. Frank Robinson was lying on the floor with the camera ready for a frog view shot. My task was to write beautiful letters with ink which dried as soon as the pen touched the slippery surface of an acetate sheet. Not an easy job at all, especially with a nervous cameraman at your feet. But with whiskey and many words of praise and encouragement toward the end, we all finished the film. It was a painful experience and I swore never to burn my fingers as a pseudo-Hollywood production manager again, but to stay with my humble pen and design alphabets.

A part of the film was made in my studio tower in Dreieichenhain, a small town between Frankfurt and Darmstadt. The tower had thick walls and dated from 1460, the year that Johannes Gutenberg printed the ›Catholicon‹ in nearby Mainz. I had once bought at auction a fragment of a sheet of this book, that was hanging in one of the rooms. (You can watch this Hallmark movie comfortably at home now, because Linotype has put it on the ›Zapfino‹ typeface CD).

Let's go back to typefaces and typography. In the 1960s the radical move from the Gutenberg principle of metal type towards other methods of typesetting production began. It started with phototypesetting and then went digital when Dr. Ing. Rudolf Hell in Kiel/Germany invented the ›Digiset‹ composing machine in 1964. I have witnessed and participated in all these stages of type production; from hot metal composition in the 1950s, then phototypesetting, and now digital methods. It's been an exciting time with all the dramatic changes that the printing industry has seen, especially in the last 30 years.

Typographic Variations

In 1963, at the time when photocomposition was gradually displacing metal type, a fine specimen of letterpress was done at the house printing office of the D. Stempel AG typefoundry, containing many examples of my book designs over the past years. This was ›Typographic Variations‹, a book composed of 78 book- and title pages designed on themes in contemporary book design and typography, with prefaces by G. K. Schauer, Frankfurt; Paul Standard, New York; and Charles Peignot, Paris; together with commentary notes and specifications. The German edition was published in 1963 by Georg Kurt Schauer in Frankfurt, the American edition in 1964 by Museum Books, Inc. in New York, and the French edition in 1965 by Hermann (Pierre Berès) éditeurs des sciences et des arts in Paris. The next page shows two examples from ›Typographic Variations‹ (reduced).

Amerikanisches
Theater *4 Theaterstücke*

EUGENE O'NEILL *Seite 9*
Ein Mond für die Beladenen

THORNTON WILDER *117*
Unsere kleine Stadt

TENNESSEE WILLIAMS *191*
Die Katze auf dem heißen Blechdach

ARTHUR MILLER *287*
Der Tod des Handlungsreisenden

Mit einem Nachwort von S. Melchinger

Büchergilde Gutenberg Frankfurt/Main

Since the early 1960s I have been working on the use of typography in computer programs. When you are a book designer you are always looking for ways of simplifying production. In particular, you need precise typesetting specifications, for which I became well-known among the publishers. But there was room for improvement in the technical process. At first my ideas about computer-aided typesetting were not taken seriously in Germany and were called futuristic fantasies. They were even rejected at the Technische Hochschule in Darmstadt, where I lectured in typography from 1972 to 1981. The director of a big company – which is no longer in existence – thought that it was unrealistic to apply modular structures to typesetting with the aid of a computer. »That Zapf is crazy«, he said, as I later discovered from his secretary, »he should stick with alphabets«.

Of course nobody could have predicted that computerized typography would become the order of the day a few years later. In these days computers are everywhere. Even children of pre-school age are playing with them. Today, modern life without computers is unthinkable.

Since nobody wanted to hear about my ideas in Germany, I had no choice but to go to the United States. The Americans were more open to such new and unconventional things, as they still have something of their old pioneering spirit. For my lectures there I developed my ideas about computerized typesetting programs. My moment came when I was invited to speak to the students at the Carpenter Center for the Visual Arts at Harvard University in Cambridge/Massachusetts on October 27, 1964.

»In about the year 1957, a new development in typography almost coincided with the launching of the first space satellite. Lead, which is heavy and earthbound, was challenged by photocomposition – a phenomenon similar to the victory over gravity. The coincidence is striking and deserves some reflection.

The age of electronics has brought the second industrial revolution. Can we, in the graphics trade, keep pace with these rapid developments? Computers, and with them automatic typesetting, are now invading our composing rooms. They take no heed of tradition or of craftsmanship. The printing trade has entered a new era. But many typefounders still close their eyes to this change. They continue to produce script and fancy brush faces and neglect the fact that photocomposition does this much better today.

The invention of photography in the nineteenth century had consequences similar to those following the invention of typecasting in the fifteenth century. Today photocomposition is about to replace conventional lead composition in many important fields. Photography will influence letterforms just as typecasting influenced the calligraphy of the medieval monks. For centuries, letterforms have been determined by tools and materials. Punches cut by hand produced the characteristic form that we still admire, for example, in the Garamond typefaces. Up to the beginning of the nineteenth century, printing was done on a wooden handpress. Type was made for this purpose and the technical possibilities of the particular time. Basically, there was little change within the first 400 years since the invention of typecasting by Johannes Gutenberg in Mainz.

The designer of typefaces today finds himself constantly confronted with new tasks. He must submit to conditions that have changed. In the future, too, readability must come first; it must, as long as the written word is to be read and comprehended by the human eye. Although reading machines – yes, they are with us already – require the forms of the alphabet, they will ultimately make laws of their own. No longer will the designer alone be able to solve the problems of form. Like the punchcutter of old, the electronics technician will become the designer's indispensable colleague. Increasingly, the type designer's task will be to coordinate traditional methods with modern needs.

Here is the core of the problem to come: we must have new designers to create what I would call ›programmed photo-typography‹, which will consist of several grid systems with simple variations – to avoid monotony – for use in setting the type for different books. We need no longer copy the books of early centuries; designers must set new standards so that in a few years the author's typewritten page can be given directly to the computer for typesetting.

Today it is possible to produce entire books by computers. The text is directly supplied from the computer into high-speed photocomposing machines. The make-up is pre-programmed. Without photocomposition, such jobs could never be handled with such speed. In addition, computers have tremendous capacity for variation. This enormous variety of possibilities should stimulate our imaginations as designers and lead us to new thoughts, new considerations. Computerized composition with pre-programmed details requires new thinking in terms of phototypography. Fortunately, not everything in the future will be made with the computer. The invention of the typesetting machine did not completely push aside hand composition. We must not think exclusively in the direction of complicated machinery. Let us look at modern typography from the positive angle. Photocomposition will bring new and additional possibilities. It will not radically suppress fine type design. Tasks will only shift. This is not the first instance of change within 500 years of printing history.

The new and additional possibilities of photocomposition can be seen most clearly in advertising, which today depends on differentiation. Uniformity in advertising is not possible, since it is the aim everywhere to differentiate and to simplify complex matters. Printed materials will not all be uniform although it looks sometimes as if there is a tendency to use sans serif faces for books and everything.

In book printing as well as in typography our tasks as designers will not diminish. I believe there will be a great shift from fiction, particularly cheap fiction, toward science reading. But a day will still have 24 hours. Life will be more complicated in the future. There will be many technical aids including computers for small and medium-sized tasks. You know from your daily experiences that we have to come down to the essentials. The time problem is paramount. This means necessarily a selection in our reading. New forms of textbooks, quite different from textbooks we use today, may be developed in the future.

Whether we like it or not, we have to manage the situation. Each generation has to tackle its problems. Electronics will soon force its claims upon letterforms. We must master this development – this is, I believe, our responsibility toward the future«. (From: ›Hermann Zapf and his design philosophy‹. Society of Typographic Arts, Chicago 1987. Abridged).

These were thoughts 20 years before Steve Jobs in California presented the first Macintosh computer to experts. Already in 1965, only one year after my Harvard talk, I got the chance to try a practical application of my ideas for computer-aided composition. I started early experiments in computerized typography with Dale Robinson, owner of a typesetting service in Merriam/Kansas. We attempted to configure a program for automatic spacing of capital letters on his IBM 1130 computer. The key to our counting system is shown on page 58 of ›ABC-XYZapf‹, Wynkyn de Worde Society, London, 1989.

Program IBM 1130

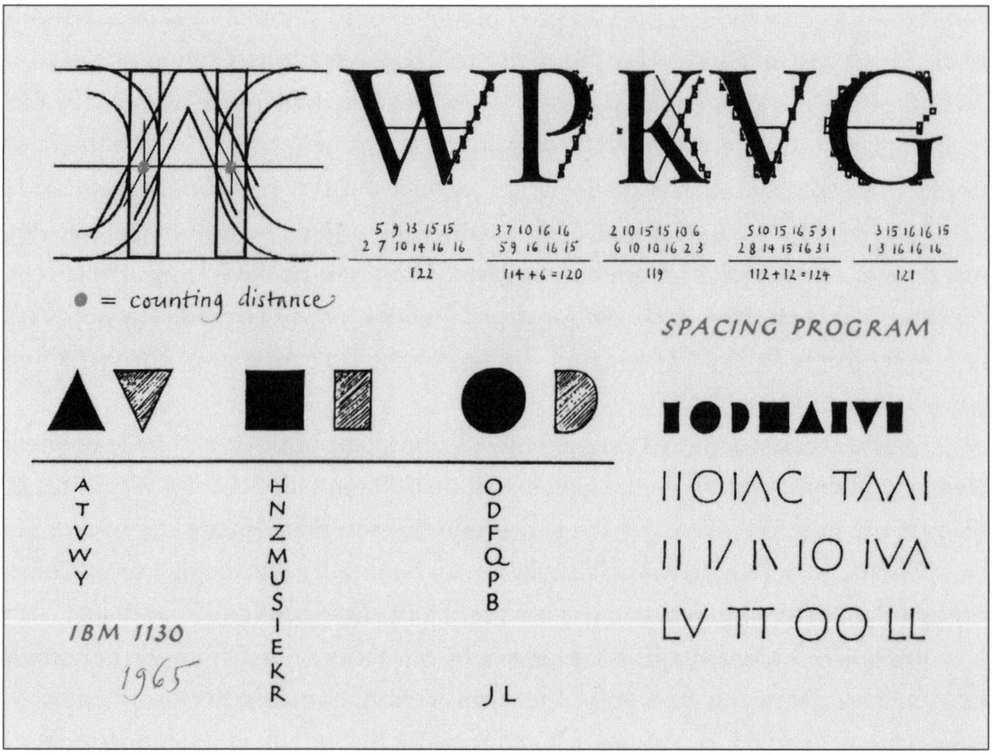

Hallmark Cards, Inc., Kansas City/Missouri, learned about our aims and got interested in these developments of integrating a computer in quality text composition. While I was a consultant to Hallmark in 1966, we started considering how to achieve efficient computer-aided book production by analyzing and experimenting with the production cycle on the ›Crown Edition‹, a series of stylish literary texts. To simplify the process and reduce the number of repeating steps in composition, diagrams were worked out to support various type sizes and type areas within the given standard size of the books. This process was supported by the computer installation at Hallmark. (An example of the research is also shown in ›ABC-XYZapf: Fifty years in alphabet design‹, Wynkyn de Worde Society, London, 1989, page 69).

During this period of my engagement with sophisticated computer programs, I was also planning a third edition of the Manuale as ›Manuale Photo-Typographicum‹ with 100 examples. The Manuale of 1954 was completely done by hand-composition, while the Manuale of 1968 was done partly by hand-composition and partly by Monotype and Linotype machine typesetting with two pages composed with alphabets from Photo-Lettering, Inc. (Edward Rondthaler) in New York. But both editions had been printed by letterpress. The ›Manuale Photo-Typographicum‹ was scheduled to be printed by the offset process with photographic illustrations of people reading. All pages were arranged within modules of a flexible grid, and were intended as examples of programmed composition. All the sizes of the photographic illustrations were standardized in modular bricks. The project was started in 1967, but for financial reasons it never got completely off the ground. The basic concept was a structure of asymmetric grid modules using the so-called Fibonacci numbers 1-1-2-3-5 (vertical) and 3-5-8 (horizontal). A proof page from the ›Manuale Photo-Typographicum‹ showing the modular elements is reproduced on page 121.

The landing on the moon by the American astronaut Neil A. Armstrong on July 20, 1969, was the catalyst for new vitality in the sciences in America. You could still feel the enthusiasm for this big event a year later in Houston. It could also be felt in Austin, the capital of Texas, where I visited in 1970. My involvement with programmed book production had also aroused the interest of the University of Texas in Austin. I was invited to the Humanities Research Center, where they surprised me with the idea to create a special professorship. The Governor made me an ›Honorary Citizen of Texas‹ – which might have exempted me from taxes – and presented me with a huge flag of the State of Texas that had once flown over the Capitol building in Austin. Moreover, Austin is a very attractive university town, and is nothing like the way one might otherwise picture Texas cities.

Back at home I told my wife the whole story. She listened patiently. Then she said that was all well and good, but she would never go to

Texas. Unfortunately my wife had only seen Texas from the air, when we once flew over endless oil fields on our way to San Diego. So that was the end of my Texas dream.

Since the American plan had come to nothing and our house in Frankfurt had become too small for my many books, we took an opportunity to move to Darmstadt and built a house next to the Rosenhöhe park.

Prinzessin Margaret von Hessen und bei Rhein had a plan to revive the tradition of the Ernst Ludwig Presse under the name ›Prinz Ludwig Presse‹ in memory of her husband, who died in 1966. Prof. Dolf Sternberger was to be in charge of the literary part, and I was to be responsible for equipment and typography. Unfortunately the project never got off the ground for lack of funds, and it turned out her administration had no feeling for fine books. We had all known from the start that the press would not generate any profits, but we had wanted to hold on to the tradition of the famous Ernst Ludwig Presse.

A few remarks about the history of the Ernst Ludwig Presse; it was located not too far from our new home in Darmstadt. Founded by the former Grand-Duke Ernst Ludwig von Hessen on October 11, 1907, the Ernst Ludwig Presse was one of the first private presses in Germany. Friedrich Wilhelm Kleukens (1878–1956) was the artistic director of the press; his brother Christian Heinrich Kleukens was responsible for the printing and was also the literary advisor. They published the works of William Shakespeare, the first edition of ›Das Blumenbuch‹ by Rudolf Koch and Fritz Kredel (printed 1929–1930), and many other books. The Ernst Ludwig Presse was one of the finest private presses in Germany, and it would have been hard for us to compete.

The model for the Prinz Ludwig Presse was a private press edition published in 1966 by the Carl Hanser Verlag in Munich: Torquato Tasso's ›Amyntas‹. This work was translated by Hanns Studniczka, and the text was printed at the Eggebrecht Presse in Mainz in the Diotima typeface designed by Gudrun. The eight etchings by Bruno Cassinari were done at Giovanni Mardersteig's ›Officina Bodoni‹ in Verona.

Some years after the failure of the Prinz Ludwig Presse project, two special private publications were printed in letterpress for I.K.H. Prinzessin Margaret von Hessen und bei Rhein. The first was done in 1977: ›Horaz, Zwölf Oden, Lateinisch und Deutsch‹, translated by Golo Mann and set in Georg Trump's Delphin type; and the second was done eight years later in 1985: ›Antonio Machado, Gedichte, Spanisch und Deutsch‹, set in Bodoni Roman and printed in an edition of 100 copies.

After my experience with the Prinz Ludwig Presse in Darmstadt, I once again put my ambitions and efforts into new projects in the United States. Ever since my time working in the ›Haus zum Fürsteneck‹, I have had a close connection with letterpress printing and the art of Johannes Gutenberg. In the late 1970s, I got the chance to participate in a rather complicated undertaking in experimental typography with an American private press printer. This was the adventure of ›Orbis Typographicus. Thoughts, words and phrases on the arts and sciences‹. Published and printed by the Crabgrass Press in Prairie Village (near Kansas City), finished in 1980. It was dedicated to Paul Standard of New York as a token of friendship. Here is the announcement by Phil Metzger:

»ORBIS TYPOGRAPHICUS. Over the past ten years, Hermann Zapf as designer and Philip Metzger as printer have worked together on the production of this portfolio of twenty-five quotations. It has been a happy collaboration motivated by a mutual interest in how hand-set type looks as printed on a hand press, and for

DON'TBALWAYSYTHINKFAHEAD
THERVERYAMOMENTNONLYZISPIMPORTANT
FORATHISHISNOUREREALMLIFE

LIFEBISYTOOFSHORT
TORLOSEAONENDAYZNONSENSICALLY
ITPMAYABEHYOURNLASTEDAYMANYWAY

sheer pleasure, as each of them has found the time to work on it. The quotations are from the writings of Thomas Alva Edison, Albert Einstein, Robert Oppenheimer, William Shakespeare, George Bernard Shaw, and such whose comments on the arts and sciences seem especially apt. The type faces used more or less in experimental typography come from the cases of the Crabgrass Press. All but a few are printed on mould-made and hand-made papers from England, France, Germany, Italy and Japan and, in three cases, from the United States: two on Worthy Hand & Arrow paper, which has not been made for years, and one on a sheet by James Yarnell of Wichita/Kansas specially for this undertaking. Most are printed in two or more colors.

The twenty-five 9x12 inch sheets and those for the title and colophon, and another giving details of production, are enclosed in a specially made Plexiglas frame allowing one to be displayed and the rest to be stored behind. The frame may be hung on a wall, or placed on edge or laid flat on a table. In addition, the inner mailing case is designed as a solander with an identifying label on one edge so the portfolio may be stored on a book shelf. Ninety-nine sets were printed of which seventy are for sale«.

Unfortunately on September 17, 1981, Phil Metzger passed away too early; he was only 67 years of age.

Another project several years later – also done in letterpress – was ›Poetry through typography: Poems selected by Walter Schmiele and Peter Frank. Introduction by Walter Schmiele and Hermann Zapf. Printed in memory of Phil Metzger (1914–1981)‹. It was published in a limited edition of only 99 copies by the Kelly-Winterton Press, New York, in 1993.

The publication contains twelve accordion-fold sheets, 13.5 x 21 cm, intended to be displayed individually by standing them on edge. The sheets are contained in a traycase made by Willy Pingel in Heidelberg. They were composed from an assortment of typefaces and printed on different papers. The examples were made with Martino Mardersteig, Verona; Sebastian Carter, Cambridge/England; Ludwig Oehms, Frankfurt; Klaus Hoffmann, Darmstadt; Walter Hamady, Mt. Horeb/Wisconsin; Jim Yarnell, Wichita/Kansas; and Jerry Kelly, New York. A specially made paper by Jim Yarnell included colored letters embedded in the paper pulp during manufacture in his little paper mill.

My introduction about the typographic arrangement of poetry follows:

»TYPOGRAPHY – next to calligraphy – is the most satisfying visible interpretation of language, of the words of a poet. Poetry may be represented in a cool, impersonal and restrained manner, or expressed with vigor and virile power. The reader should not just absorb the words silently with his eyes; no, he should be invited by the typographic arrangement of a poem to read lines out loud, especially when they appear in larger type sizes than usual or when he is in the company of friends.

The poems in this publication are designed in such a way as to permit them to stand individually on a desk for a few days; the message of some may speak quietly of an unusual situation in the reader's life and be accepted as a silent compassion, or as consolation. Is this not the most gratifying way of getting the words of a poet into your memory?

POETRY is painting with words of different shades, gently and steadily and their typographic arrangement may be viewed as an additional aid to explanation and understanding. Poetry is the peak of literature, for it is the most sensitive and personal means we know of showing innermost thoughts and feelings. A good design will help by stimulating the reader to become involved with poetry.«

Once I had some plans of my own to print books on a handpress. In 1955, I bought a beautiful old press from Stempel, since they needed to clear space in the printing office. It was a very heavy press built in 1835 at the Dingler machine factory in Zweibrücken in the Palatinate. I learned that my press was one of the last of its kind manufactured with a big oak base, and the press was much stronger than the Dingler press that Giovanni Mardersteig used at his Officina Bodoni in Verona.

My idea was originally to print limited editions composed in my Palatino under the imprint of ›Z-Presse‹ after my retirement. But a graphic designer or a painter will never retire and does not drop his pencil as soon as he becomes 65. Everything needed to run a private press was ready to start. Only one sheet in an edition of 20 was ever printed. The press located in my studio reminds me every day of the glorious days of Gutenberg's invention. It was just a dream long before the digital revolution started in the world of printing. I have been occupied with too many things since the 1960s.

But the time of metal type was fading out. In the 1960s the new digital method of text production began with the ›Digiset‹ photocomposing machine. Dr. Ing. Rudolf Hell first presented his invention to a very skep-

G. W. Leibniz

tical audience of experts in 1965 at the printing exhibition in Paris. The digital generation of letterforms was something that interested me immensely, for even at that time I was engaged with studying the binary system of notation used by Gottfried Wilhelm Leibniz (1646–1716). He was the father of the counting structure used by our computers today. (A reproduction of a special printed broadside in honor of Leibniz is shown on page 125).

Many years later Dr. Hell still remembered me, that fellow in the audience at his presentation in Paris with persistent questions about the image and design details of digital printouts. The Digiset was certainly in its infancy and produced letters that looked very primitive, particularly the way diagonal strokes had a sawtooth pattern.

Dr. Ing. Rudolf Hell

But it was only a matter of time before letters would be smooth and perfect. Dr. Hell's invention of the ›light dot‹ to generate letters was so revolutionary and different for us type designers. My co-operation with the firm called Dr. Ing. Rudolf Hell GmbH started in 1973. We did not have a monitor on which to draw or adjust the type designs; instead each letter had to be made with white paint on a pre-printed black raster sheet, totaling thousands of tiny squares. My wife helped me with this strenuous work for weeks.

Over the years the rasterization of digital letters got finer and finer, and today you don't see the single light dot anymore. Dr. Hell's digital invention not only changed typesetting, but it was instrumental to the whole art of printing by digital processes. Later, film cameras were replaced by digital cameras, and there are many other new inventions that are digital, like telefax and text transmissions over the internet. We take this for granted now and we rarely think about the digital nature of so much equipment.

Edison

For Dr. Ing. Rudolf Hell GmbH I designed five alphabets for digital generation. The first was ›Marconi Roman‹. It began in 1973 and was not finished until 1976, for I had no experience in this absolutely new media. The next was ›Edison Roman‹, a sturdy typeface tailored for newspaper typesetting and the conditions of high-speed rotary presses. This was followed by ›Digiset Vario‹, a brush type for headlines. Between 1981 and 1983, I worked on ›Aurelia Roman‹, which was planned to be a classic roman that would work for book production. The goal of this commission was to make a typeface inspired by Nicolas Jenson's roman of 1470,

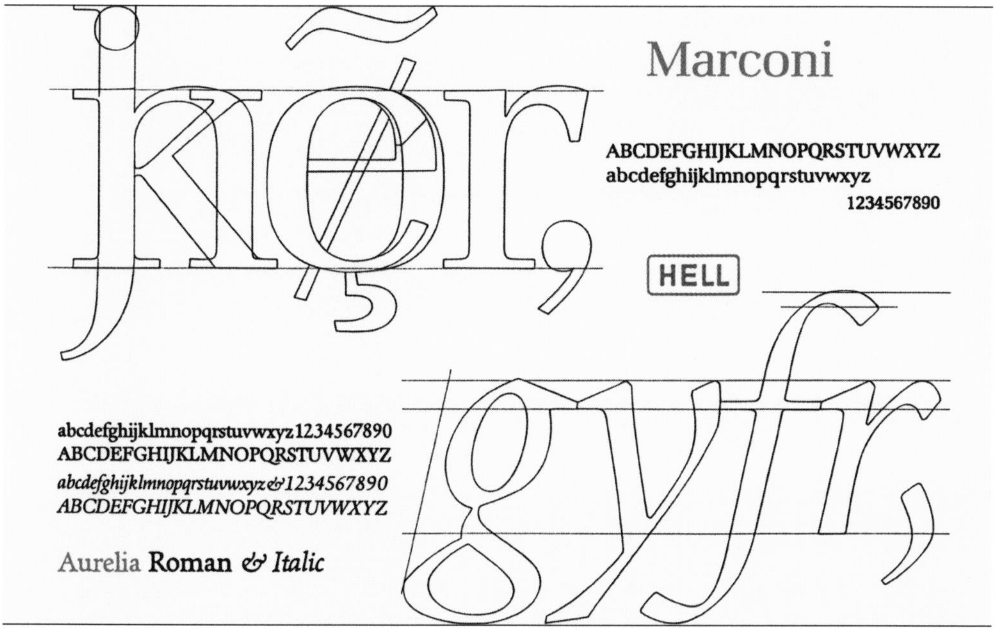

but not to make a copy; rather it was to be a modern interpretation as a digital typeface. I was also commissioned to design the special type for World Book, Inc. (Chicago, London, Sydney, and Toronto) for use on the American Digiset machine produced by RCA. They wanted a text face similar to ›Optima Roman‹ with an electronically obliqued italic. It was named ›World Book Modern‹ and was first used in 1992 for the 75th Jubilee Edition of the ›World Book Encyclopedia‹ in 22 volumes.

The war in Vietnam finally ended in 1975. Soldiers from the United States had been fighting in Vietnam since the late 1950s. The names of more

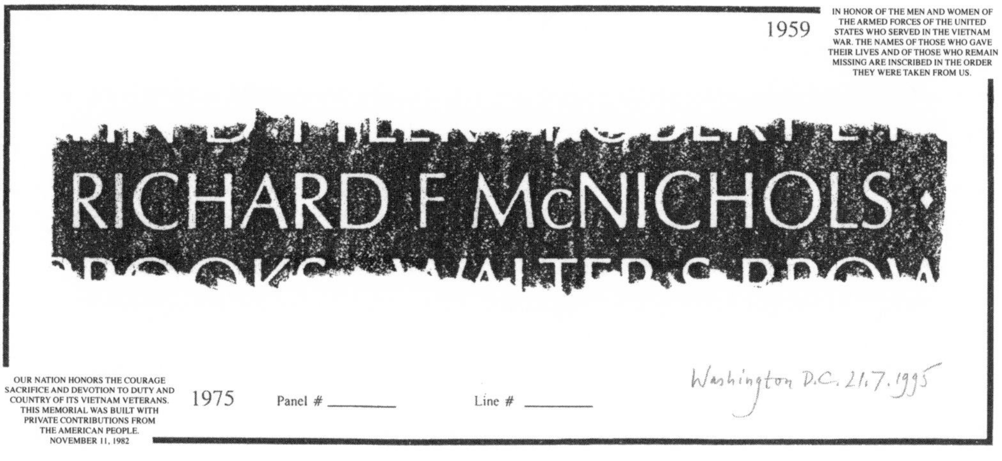

than 58,000 American soldiers who died in this war are on the Vietnam Veterans Memorial in Washington D.C. This monument was designed by Maya Lin, and the names were inscribed on black granite in the Optima typeface. Everyone now hoped for a peaceful future after this disaster, and it was a great relief for the American students.

In 1976 I was invited to a meeting with Dean Mark Guldin and Prof. Alexander S. Lawson from the School of Printing Management and Sciences at the Rochester Institute of Technology (RIT) in Rochester/New York. I was asked if I would teach when Prof. Lawson retired. They wanted to set up a special professorship for typographic computer programs, the first of its kind in the world. Here is RIT's announcement (abridged) of my courses that started in June of 1977:

»TYPOGRAPHIC COMPUTER PROGRAMS (FORMATTING): The course objective is the development of special grid and modular programs (formats) for all kinds of typographic variations that are tailored for economic book/magazine design and production. This is an advanced study course exploring the new structures of formatting for computerized photocomposition. Projects explore the possibilities of raising design standards and reducing costs for complicated composition work by using grid structures and computer programs. The course is specifically designed to focus on essential information for the organization of production. The course will not deal with computerized newspaper page make-up. Course includes lectures and laboratory exercises.

ALPHABET DESIGN FOR PHOTOCOMPOSITION: This course will focus on the development of types in the USA, Europe, and Japan since 1947 (the year Frederic W. Goudy died); and will link historic typefaces with the new challenges of today. The course includes discussion of alphabet designs for digital storage; analysis of computer assisted drawings and modifications; and critical studies of alphabets used on photocomposition systems today. Students will analyze technical parameters of designs for both existing and future photocomposition equipment, and will discuss how to get better composition quality.

ADVANCED CALLIGRAPHY: This is a course in calligraphy and lettering for commercial use. Exercises include the study of different alphabets; the use of new tools and time saving methods; and letter design with the broad-edged pen and pointed brush. This workshop is not for beginners in calligraphy, but is intended especially for graphic designers and lettering artists who want to further develop their skills. Emphasis is on individual assistance. The class is limited to a maximum of 16 people in order to make this course more beneficial to participants and to allow teacher-student demonstrations and active dialogue with the teacher.«

I taught at RIT from 1977 to 1987, flying back and forth between Darmstadt and Rochester. It would have been so convenient for me to teach typographic computer programs in Darmstadt; I could have walked from my home to the Technische Hochschule nearby. But in Rochester I had the chance to develop my ideas further, particularly once I made contacts with companies like IBM and Xerox through my students. I also learned a great deal from the computer specialists during our discussions, which often continued into the night. More and more I realized how necessary it was to have a hand in the new technical developments, and not leave everything to the computer engineers.

I made contacts at the Rochester Institute of Technology as early as the 1950s, and connections were particularly strong after I received RIT's Frederic W. Goudy Award in 1969. (My wife Gudrun was honored with the same distinction in 1998, which was very unusual). During these years I developed a strong interest in the holdings of the Melbert B. Cary, Jr. Graphic Arts Collection, which was located on the campus. The collection was named after Mr. Cary, former director of the Continental Type Founders Association, and an avid book collector. He had also been the American agent for the Gebr. Klingspor typefoundry in Offenbach. The Cary Collection is dedicated to the memory of Frederic W. Goudy, the American type designer who lived from 1865 to 1947. I have known just about all the great heroes of the graphic arts in the 20th century, except (unfortunately) Rudolf Koch and Frederic W. Goudy.

Sequoyah Syllabary

During the time I was teaching at RIT, I received a very interesting commission from Prof. Walter Hamady from the University of Wisconsin in Madison. It was the redesign of the historic ›Sequoyah Syllabary‹ of the Cherokee Indians. This type consisted of 85 signs developed by Chief Sequoyah over a period of 12 years. His alphabet was adopted by the Cherokee Nation in 1821. It was used for religious publications and to produce the ›Cherokee Phoenix‹ newspaper. The Sequoyah Syllabary had very unusual letterforms without a system and structure, a mixture of roman letters and Sequoyah's inventions. Our redesign was intended to be printed along with Monotype Walbaum and was therefore designed to work with the Monotype unit system. After four years of research my

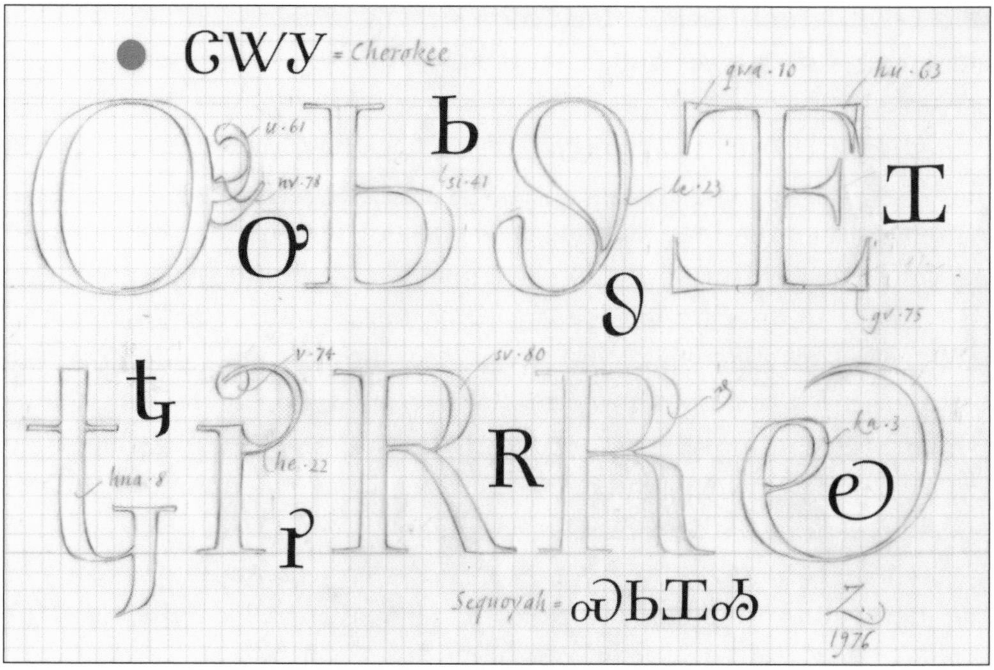

drawings were finished in 1977, but it was not until 1984 that we were able to show the first text examples. In the meantime, metal typesetting was dying out. A digital version had to be worked out. During the years of this project, I had a great opportunity to study the history of the American Indians, their culture, and their sad destiny.

Design Processing International

In 1977, my friends Aaron Burns and Herb Lubalin joined me in founding ›Design Processing International, Incorporated‹ (DPI) in New York. Our aim was to develop programs for typographic structures based on a variable menu, to be used by non-specialists such as office workers and secretaries (Aaron Burns referred to such users as ›typographists‹). For me, it was also a chance to apply the substance of my RIT lectures in practical conditions. But at DPI, we didn't want to find typographic solutions so that amateurs could work in the printing industry; instead, at that time our target was the office market and the operators of so-called word processing systems. Our concept was based on printed menus. The user could select from various typographic possibilities and mix different options. By applying the appropriate DPI codes to selections, the user would produce precisely tailored outputs. My instruments were module-based instruction books with pages cut horizontally through the middle so the user could turn back and forth to find the best combination to suit his or her imagination. (Some examples are shown in ›Hermann Zapf and his design philosophy‹, Society of Typographic Arts, Chicago, 1987, pages 236–237).

These modular composition bricks allowed hundreds of variable solutions for brochures, dissertations, in-house magazines and annual reports. We also had an aim at DPI to get away from the old terms of metal type like leading, point sizes, kerned letters, etc. The special feature of our system was the automatic arrangement of type sizes for headlines in a given width. This was one of the ways our system helped ordinary office workers without typographic know-how. The DPI concept was that it should be as simple as possible to make good typographic layouts.

The technical developments in personal computers went on. A new milestone was the introduction in 1984 of a truly practical system in the Macintosh computer, developed at Apple, the company founded by Steve Jobs and Steve Wozniak. The direct presentation on the monitor and the easy maneuvering with the electronic mouse were very different from our concept of selecting various components within the printed DPI manuals. Secretaries were not Apple's target group; instead, right from the start, they were dedicated to providing professional solutions and nothing less.

In September of 1984 I received a Mac as a gift from Steve Jobs of Apple Computer, Inc. It was one of the early computers manufactured in Cupertino/California. In those early days a Mac was still something quite uncommon, and you could carry the 128k Mac wherever you like in a soft carrying bag.

A little story belongs here. Late one evening I received a telephone call from a person named Tom Suiter. He told me his boss had given him a list of ten names starting with Woody Allen and ending with mine (A to Z). Each was to receive an Apple computer. Of course, at the beginning of the conversation I was a little skeptical, for it was not the time of Santa Claus, and we at DPI did not have any connection with Apple Computer in Cupertino. But the computer arrived, and after everything was installed I had a lot of trouble with my new electronic tool. My first trials drove me to despair, especially when my laboriously designed examples suddenly caused a crash and I had to call Cupertino to get assistance and new courage. At that time, there was no regular help hotline.

The following year Design Processing International was invited to Cupertino. In the presence of Steve Jobs, I explained our menu concept with slides. He was in Levi's, and Aaron and I were dressed in such a distinguished manner that we looked like we were on our way to a funeral. To tell the truth, at the end it was a farewell to some of our thoughts of entering the professional territory in the future with our DPI instruction books and solutions defined by codes. We explained our latest and most sophisticated DPI system that integrated a monitor with a word processor. Here are a few thoughts from the presentation I gave in the Apple conference room on April 25, 1985.

»At Design Processing International we are not talking about ›9-point‹ anymore, nor using words like ›lowercase‹, for these are anachronisms in the digital age. We are talking about size 9, type size 10, etc. This is because the DPI Menu Manuals with simplified printer terms and the simplified code system are meant to be used by everybody, even those without any typographic background.

The idea is like picking flowers in a garden center. You don't know the botanical names, all the species, or the hybrids. You select them because you like them for their colors. This is our DPI principle for we do not want to bother our user with unfamiliar typographic terms.

Another feature: we can specify the same code no matter what the term or language. As an example, take the code ›type style‹. You can say – if you don't know the correct name – typeface, alphabet, type style, font, type (English); or Schrift, Buchstaben, Typen (German); or skrifter (Swedish); or pismo (Czech); or caractére, lettres (French); etc., etc. But it always means the same thing, and the computer will select the typeface, even if called by different names. The same will be done with other instruction terms. These days, it is a simple programming solution on a chip. All this is inside the DPI system and no extra hardware is required«. (Abridged).

After our visit to Cupertino, we concentrated our subsequent efforts on the office market only, and we stayed with our example booklets that were each tailored for different solutions. Design Processing International existed until 1986. Herb Lubalin died suddenly on May 29, 1981 (he was my age, born in 1918).

We set up Zapf, Burns & Company in New York at Hammarskjold Plaza in 1987. We adjusted to the new technical developments directed by Apple, and our new concept was based on ›ab-z styles‹ (Aaron Burns-

Zapf). We didn't want to copy the Apple design philosophy, but we did want to concentrate on a visual presentation of typographic design solutions and combinations.

Sadly, in 1991 my partner Aaron Burns died of AIDS, which he had contracted from a blood transfusion during a heart bypass operation in 1982. He had been responsible for our marketing. To add to his troubles, two of our employees had stolen my ideas and started a company of their own shortly before his death. That was the last straw for Aaron, and a terrible experience for both of us. Of course, it was not practical for me to run a company in the USA from Darmstadt. I couldn't even take legal action, and I didn't want to move to New York. Anyone who has seen our house on the Rosenhöhe in Darmstadt will understand why.

Independent of all these connections with the computer world, I was still interested in calligraphy, partly because I was teaching calligraphy at Rochester Institute of Technology. The appreciation of calligraphy as an artistic expression in society, like painting and photography, was of special interest to me at that time.

The manifesto ›The calligrapher in our time‹ was written in 1984 for the Society of Scribes and Illuminators in London.

»We don't create heroic things to earn fame. We put no scratches on the globe, but perhaps with our gentle art we add a few little dabs of joy to life, as in a nicely written praise of the Lord, written with the complete engagement of our heart. Calligraphy is a peaceful and noble art, done by well-educated human beings who do their work with full commitment, with intense concentration. For we want to put into our letters a little of our own feeling, of our personality and mood. Letters should have grace and beauty in themselves. We see everywhere a growing interest in calligraphy. In the future people will work fewer hours a day and hopefully some may use their free time to do something creative with their hands.

A few more facts about calligraphers. No calligrapher pollutes rivers with his ink, or poisons the air we breathe. Calligraphy makes no noise. We don't fight with arms nor with our pens, but we sometimes want to convince with a hand-lettered message of special importance in which we believe. Of course we know we are not the center of the world – we merely like to make nice things with our given talent. And we have a burden of responsibility: the heritage of the great masters of the past, the tradition of the scribes of the Middle Ages, the memory of our royal and imperial ancestors in Europe and Asia. Calligraphy is still a royal activity«.

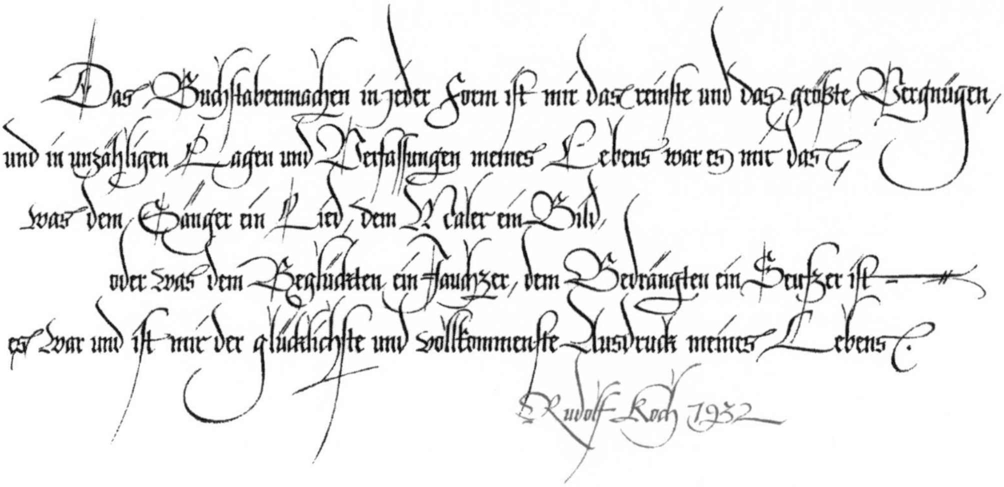
Das Buchstabenmachen in jeder Form ist mir das reinste und das größte Vergnügen,
und in unzähligen Lagen und Verfassungen meines Lebens war es mir das,
was dem Sänger ein Lied, dem Maler ein Bild,
oder was dem Beglückten ein Jauchzer, dem Bedrängten ein Seufzer ist —
es war und ist mir der glücklichste und vollkommenste Ausdruck meines Lebens.
Rudolf Koch 1932

A strong calligraphic influence from calligraphy can be seen in a typeface named ›AMS-Euler‹ that was created for the typesetting of mathematical books and documents. It may look very unusual, but from the beginning the intention of this typeface was to depart from the cool representation of mathematics and to attempt a more human expression. The Euler project was started in the 1980s with Prof. Donald E. Knuth of the Computer Science Department at Stanford University, and was developed for the American Mathematical Society (AMS) in Providence/Rhode Island. AMS-Euler was named in honor of Leonhard Euler (1707–1783), a Swiss mathematician who lived and worked primarily in St. Petersburg/Russia.

Don Knuth suggested a more handwritten look for the letterforms, much like the way formulas are written by mathematicians. For inspiration we studied the handwriting of Leonhard Euler from some of his St. Petersburg records, and also the handwriting of Albert Einstein. The drop-shaped figure zero is characteristic of the AMS-Euler design. The 0 has a special shape to clearly distinguish it from the letter o. The original idea was to finish the different AMS-Euler alphabets (totaling nearly 500 letterforms) in 1983, because this was the 200th anniversary of Leonard Euler's death.

David Siegel, who was a student at Stanford and helped with the digitizing of the Euler alphabets, published a description of the typeface. Here is an excerpt from ›The Euler Project at Stanford‹, Department of Computer Science, Stanford University 1985. (Abridged):

»The Euler Project traces its beginnings to 1979, when Donald Knuth of Stanford University completed a book called ›TeX and METAFONT, New Directions in Typesetting‹. In this book, he described two programs he had developed for producing technical reports on computer driven printers. TEX, a text formatting language, gave authors the ability to typeset mathematics and technical material easily and inexpensively. METAFONT makes fonts for programs such as TEX to use in making pages for books, journals, etc.

The American Mathematical Society began using TEX to set journal articles in Computer Modern, a typeface designed by Knuth using METAFONT. Computer Modern has a special math italic character set for use in TEX's math mode. This font had so many math characters, it was immediately accepted by those who had spent much time trying to fish characters out of strange fonts for their notation. However, mathematicians frequently use bold or italic letters for emphasis. Set in Computer Modern math italic, Euler's famous equation $e^{i\pi}+1=0$, might not look as elegant as it really is.

Knuth wanted a typeface that would be more distinguishable from text, yet familiar to mathematicians. He wanted letters that were consistent, but not dry. After all, his goal is to share the beauty and enjoyment of mathematics with those who care to read his books.

In 1980, Knuth collaborated with the German type designer Hermann Zapf to provide the world with a typeface for use in equations of mathematical texts. The mathematician turned printer and the typographer turned scientist proposed to the AMS an upright cursive design to solve this problem.

In selecting this rather unconservative style for a mathematics face, they argued that it should be professionally drawn to meet the following criteria:

– Neither weight nor slant should distinguish it from text, since mathematicians use both in text and equations for special meanings and emphasis.

– A handwritten, yet consistent, appearance would suit equations, since formulas are usually handwritten rather than typewritten.

– A math character set must include all the alphabets mathematicians want: Roman, Greek, Fraktur, and Script, complete with symbols, digits and punctuation.

Zapf submitted sample drawings of the new design to the Font Committee of the AMS. In addition to the upright cursive, Zapf was commissioned to draw a complete math character set in two weights: medium and bold.

The new design was a thoughtful solution, with many of the trademarks for which Zapf is famous. Even when surrounded by text, like this, $e^{i\pi}+1=0$, the Euler design brings a crisp, fresh look to old, tired expressions. Euler is the perfect typeface for any equation.

Zapf had drawn the letters with a fine ballpoint pen. When reduced, the forms had a calligraphic look. In particular, the stems were slightly tapered, to appear as though they had been drawn with a flexible pen nib that varies in width from the beginning to the end of the stroke. This style can be seen in many of his typefaces. Although Euler introduces a departure from earlier mathematical typography, the typeface attempts to satisfy as many authors and readers as possible. It may take some time to gain acceptance around the world, but it is based on firm typographic principles. Equations set in Euler must endure the smudge of the overinked press onto the flimsiest of papers. They must not fade away on the drum of a laser printer, nor under the not-so-bright lights of the ancient photocopiers of the math library, nor lose their vertical hold on the face of the CRT typesetter. The letters must not blur under the dimmest of lighting near the periodicals, through the foggiest of trifocals; they must shine clearly through the forest of hen scratchings during proofreading. They must be lucid to the last dot of an i in the most nested of subscripts, the deepest recurrence relations and under the squarest of roots. The Euler typeface is ready to meet these challenges at the AMS and, through their licensing program, in industry and universities throughout the world«.

The history of the development of AMS-Euler, including some of our correspondence, is shown in the article by Donald E. Knuth & Hermann Zapf ›AMS-Euler. A new typeface for mathematics‹ published in the journal ›Scholarly Publishing‹, Vol. 20, No. 3, Toronto, April 1989. The Euler fonts are available in the ›Gudrun & Hermann Zapf Collection‹ of 143 high quality typefaces issued by Linotype GmbH in 2003.

S:¡NEWAVE¿ SPEC.ALF. 32 Monday, September 5, 1983 17:35:14 c1390

Euler designed for the American Mathematical Society.
A system called Metafont was used to produce the bitmaps.

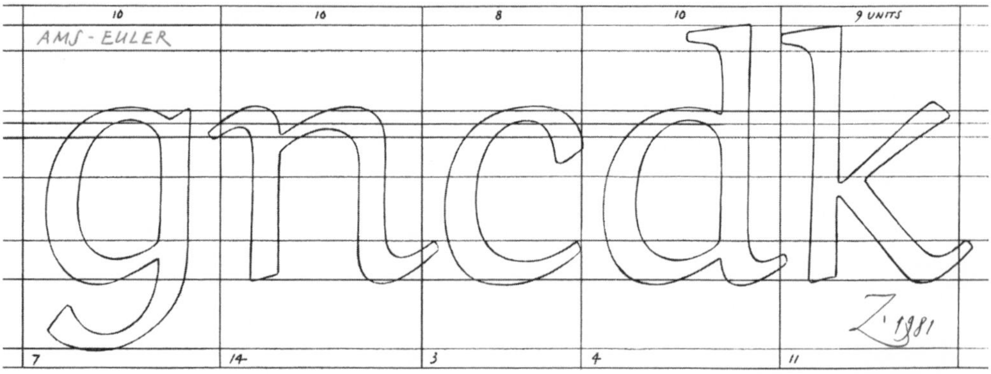

Roman Medium ABCDEFGHIJKLMNOPQURSTUVWXYZ 1234567890
abcdefghijklmnopqurstuvwxyz
Greek characters ΓΔΘΛΞΠΣΥΦΨΩαβγδεζηθικλμνξπρστυφχψωεϑϖφ

Here, another calligraphic alphabet named ›Zapf Renaissance Roman‹ should be mentioned. It was commissioned in 1984 by the firm ›Scangraphic Dr. Böger GmbH‹ in Hamburg. Their ›Scantext 1000‹ machine was a very advanced system and I could use all its technical features and my imagination within digital resolution. They wanted a book face in the direction of Palatino with many additional swash letters in the italic to demonstrate the versatility of the Scantext 1000.

With the possibilities of this equipment, you could get away from the limited standard layout of characters available in the past for the first time. I was given freedom to add what I liked into this design, such as small caps, ligatures, fleurons, etc. This was nearly ten years ahead of the OpenType format developed in the 1990s.

The Renaissance Roman is based on the ideal design proportions the artists and scholars of the 15th and 16th centuries adhered to. If you examine the lower case, you will find that the relative proportions of the ascenders and descenders to the x-height is in accordance with the ›Sectio Aurea‹, the Golden Section of the Renaissance. The proportional relationship was well known to the great early printers and punchcutters, such as Nicolas Jenson, Aldus Manutius and by Claude Garamond. The Zapf Renaissance type family does not follow, for example, the rule of aligning to the old ›German Standard Baseline‹. This particular German alignment of 1905 was based on the traditional Fraktur designs. Consequently, Roman letters had to align with Fraktur. The result was obvious – it caused all Roman faces to have short descenders, out of proportion to the x-height and the ascenders. The design was created after careful tests for book and magazine work that require a bookface to provide maximum legibility and carries none of the many technical restrictions that were (and still are) found in the classical hot metal faces and in phototypesetting.

The ›Zapf Renaissance Italic‹, designed in 1985, offers many extra letters, especially in the alternative characters of finals and ligatures. As many as four versions of a single character have been made, depending upon its possible placement in a word. The beginning and terminal character variants, together with the unusual swashes of the ascenders, can create a variable arrangement of typographic display. Since so many combinations of alternative characters are possible with the Renaissance Italic, the discipline of a discerning typographer must be exercised for a effective use of this face. (See p. 119).

I laid all the experiences I gathered over the years into developing a new and very ambitious composition program for the improvement of typesetting quality. It is named ›*hz*-Program‹ and I developed it in conjunction with URW Software & Type GmbH in Hamburg. (See p. 123). The printed announcement of the ›*hz*-Program‹ explains the basic structure and the ideas behind the concept:

hz-Program

»NON-PLUS-ULTRA TYPOGRAPHY. Phototypesetting reached today, within a few years, a standard of quality which superseded hot metal composition. The so-called kerning of difficult letter combinations is no problem at all today and is a matter of course in quality text composition. The optical margin compensation at the left and right side of text columns should also be a matter of course.

By using all the electronic possibilities within the new composition program developed by the URW Software & Type GmbH in Hamburg/Germany, optimal lines can be composed comparable with the composition of the famous 42-line Bible of Johannes Gutenberg.

Narrow spacing between words and perfectly justified lines have always been a typographic goal. In the past, to accomplish this meant an unusual investment of time resulting in increasing costs.

In his lectures about the use of typographic computer programs at the Rochester Institute of Technology, The School of Printing Management and Sciences, Hermann Zapf analyzed such typographic complexities, and since 1978 he has worked on aesthetic programs. The result of all these tests and research is now available to the typographic world in a program developed by URW. Incomparable typography is the answer, without unsightly holes within a text line, with a maximum of two consecutive hyphenated words, with almost no loss of typesetting speed, and without any additional text input effort. No complicated coding, and no need for large-scale counting methods in advance of a job. The *hz*-Program automatically finds the best solution.

As a result of studies over many years, URW's new *hz*-Program will help every photocomposition system to get type composition of the very highest quality. Try comparing conventional typography with the essentially better type areas prepared by URW's *hz*-Program.

The *hz*-Program is the key to perfection in composition, and it works no matter what typeface is chosen. It is easy to integrate the *hz*-Program in existing composition programs, it takes over the paragraph make-up, and at the same time gives optimal composition with optically balanced margins«. (From the announcement by Peter Karow, Hamburg 1990. Abridged).

The key task of the *hz*-Program is to electronically manipulate letters so they can be minutely condensed or expanded when necessary to avoid broad word spaces within a line. These tricks are done in a very subtle way so the reader doesn't recognize the changes. The announcement of the *hz*-Program showed comparisons of texts set with the *hz*-Program and without it. Here is an excerpt:

»What makes the Gutenberg Bible a great masterpiece of printing? The printing on a handpress? Not really; today's standards show us the inking was not of extraordinary quality. We could also order handmade rag paper today. Maybe the secret of his beautiful pages is in the proportions of the columns on the paper. But this we are also able to copy. Therefore, this leaves only the composition to be considered as the key factor for success.

How could Gutenberg get those even grey areas of his columns without disturbing or unsightly holes between words? His secret: the master achieved this perfection by the use of an abundance of characters he had in his type case in addition to the standard alphabetic characters; he had several alternate characters of different widths, many ligatures, and a lot of abbreviations. In total, he created 290 characters for the composition of the 42-line Bible. It must have been an enormous time-consuming job to get typographic lines: the justified lines of even length, compared to the flushleft lines in the works of the famous medieval scribes.

But today we can't use Johannes Gutenberg's unusual ligatures and abbreviations as a principle to achieve good contemporary composition. Now we can get help through the versatility of modern electronic software and formats to create a perfect type area in our production. To get closer to Gutenberg's standards of quality, use the *hz*-Program from URW«. (URW – Unternehmensberatung Karow Rubow Weber GmbH, Hamburg 1990. Abridged).

The *hz*-Program was patented by the European Patent Office in Munich on October 19, 1994. A comprehensive report on the *hz*-Program was published in the ›Seybold Report‹ in February of 1993:

»It's been a long time since we've had a really innovative approach to the handling of hyphenation and justification of text. There have been some interesting technological developments that may relate to H&J (hyphenation and justification), but nothing that presents us with a fresh, new approach in a complete package. That is what URW and type designer Hermann Zapf have done with the *hz*-Program (the *hz* being the initials of the developer).

The *hz*-Program has a lot of nice features, the target of which is to produce justified text that has nearly uniform interword spacing – no rivers of white space, no need to use letterspacing to reduce white space, no alternating tight and loose lines that distract the reader.

EVALUATION. – Even spacing. We know of no other composition program that can come anywhere near to *hz*- in producing even interword spacing over justified text, especially at this point size (9.5 points) and line measure (13.67 picas). Differences in spacing from one line to another are barely noticeable.

– Margins. Hung punctuation, if done properly, makes the left and right margins of a column appear to be straight, rather than showing obvious indentations where a tiny punctuation mark appears. The *hz*-approach is an excellent one«. (From: ›URW's *hz*-Program: Bringing Top-Quality Composition to OEMs‹ an article by Arlene E. Karch in the ›Seybold Report on Publishing Systems‹. Vol. 32, No. 11, February 22, 1993, Media/Pennsylvania. Abridged). – OEM means Original Equipment Manufacturer.

But a detailed analysis of the *hz*-Program was made by the Vietnamese typographer and computer scientist Hàn Thé Thành for his dissertation written for the Faculty of Informatics at Masaryk Universitat in Brno/Czech Republic. It is titled ›Micro-typographic extensions to the TEX typesetting system‹. Here is an excerpt:

»The *hz*-Program is the result of the research on ›micro-typography for advanced typesetting‹ by Hermann Zapf in conjunction with URW. The developers returned to printing in Gutenberg's days to find out the keys to success of the typographic masterpiece, i.e. the 42-line Bible. Some techniques used by Gutenberg, like the use of ligatures and abbreviations, were examined and later discarded. The reason is that reading habits and customs have changed from Gutenberg's time and the use of many ligatures and abbreviations that were common at that time is not acceptable today. Other techniques like multiple glyphs with varying widths or hanging punctuation turned out to be very worthwhile. The *hz*-Program, however, does not only simply follow the techniques in Gutenberg's composition. In order to gain Gutenberg's typographic standard of even interword spacing and optically straight margins, the developers introduced the ›ten typographic commandments‹, concerning three areas of typesetting: kerning, scaling and composing.

The *hz*-Program introduced three new variables for composition: improved letter spacing (kerning), typographically acceptable expansion or condensing of characters (scaling) and improved applied programming (composing). The *hz*-

Program is a set of modules for text composition that can bring these features into the H&J engine of desktop publishing systems. The modules can be used together or separately«. (Reprinted in ›TUGboat, The Communications of the $\TeX$ Users Group‹. Vol. 21, No. 4, December 2000, Portland/Oregon).

During a conference at the University Clausthal-Zellerfeld in Germany in March of 2000, I met Hàn Thé Thành personally and we talked about an extension of my *hz*-Program. I believed the existing algorithm for the horizontal expansion and condensing of letters could be improved with the addition of a vertical variant for automatic adjustment of the existing x-height. The goal: to avoid a ›widow‹, a short line at the top of a page, or an ›orphan‹, a short word or a part of a line left dangling at the end of the page, thereby cutting or adding one line to a composed page. (This method works only across a double page spread).

Zapf Dingbats

Who knows what ›dingbats‹ are? There is no better German word for this funny term than ›Krimskram‹. Dingbat comes from slang used by American compositors. In the old days of metal type, dingbats were a wild jumble of all sorts of signs, fists and of ornaments located in a corner of the typecase. Originally the incunabula printers adopted some of them from the medieval scribes; fleurons and the well-known Aldus leaf. They were used to decorate title pages or to bring attention to important words within a text. ›Zapf Dingbats‹ were originally designed in 1977 for International Typeface Corporation (ITC) in New York. During a conversation with my friends Aaron Burns and Herb Lubalin, they asked me if I could do a new typeface for ITC. A good question, and it brought to mind the collection of sketches I had drawn over many years, for about 1,200 signs, arrows and symbols. They liked the idea of a special collection of signs and symbols, and during the talk about the technical details, Ed Rondthaler at once came up with the name ›Zapf Dingbats‹. The ITC people didn't have any patience and I had to make the final drawings as quickly as possible. They wanted to release the Zapf Dingbats to their subscribers in the spring of 1978. There was no time for me to make changes in the three series or to make corrections in the designs. Herb Lubalin wanted to throw out the @-sign. Twenty-five years ago, nobody was able to foresee that the at-sign (in German ›Klammeraffe‹) would become so important one day. In general I was not happy with the Zapf Dingbats, even though they are in use worldwide today, because the ITC project was managed in such a hurry. I've had to live all these years with the result. You can't make a typeface under the pressure of time. A good work needs its time.

I always hoped to get an opportunity to improve all my dingbats. In the meantime telefax was invented, the use of mobile phones grew, e-mail happened, and the Euro symbol was invented. (See p. 130).

In late 2001, Linotype GmbH in Bad Homburg/Germany published a collection of digital dingbats and ornaments with the name ›Zapf Essentials‹, designed for everyday use (and as the name says, you just have to have them). There are endless possibilities for their use, as the font contains 372 designs with a variety of current and updated symbols. In addition to monetary signs, there are quick arrows with fading tails to show speed, and arrows with reminder knots. ›Zapf Essentials‹ contains a large number of categories. In alphabetical order, they are: adornments, Aldus leaves, arrows, boxes, bullets, currency signs, cutters, decorations, and emphasizers, extras, eyecatchers, fillers, fingers, fleurons, flourishes, geometrical elements, glyphs, hands (feminine and masculine), icons, indexes, indicators, markers, ornaments, pointers, scissors, separators, shouters, signals, signs, stars, symbols, three-dimensional signs, etc.

The Zapf Essentials should be used sparingly to highlight important parts of a text. There are no limits to the user's imagination in playing with these signs and symbols, and I hope everyone has as much fun as I had during the time I worked on the improvement of the old gray dingbats.

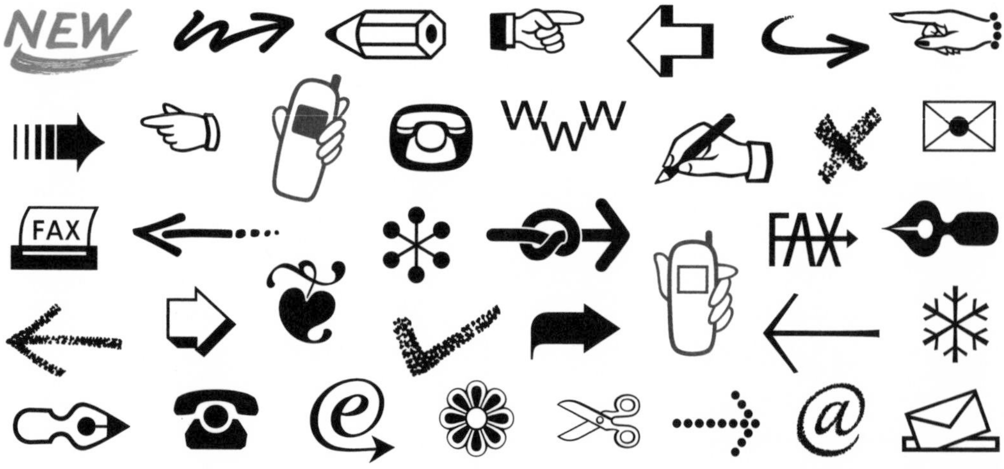

In the time of metal types, the expense to produce a new typeface was so enormous that typefounders were very careful about starting new designs. Also in the old days a typographer could memorize the most important alphabets on the market. That era is over. The inflation of altered typefaces brings the number on today's market to more than 10,000 alphabets. It is now quite easy to make a new typeface with the aid of a computer. Of course not all these creations are truly new designs, perhaps some are warmed over versions or manipulations of existing alphabets or look-alikes of doubtful origin.

The shady side of type design is the copying of alphabets. Unfortunately, the Palatino font has the sad distinction of being the most copied typeface in the world. One day there was a call for the foundation of an organization for a very special group of people. Here is the text of the resolution:

»It's high time to establish a ›Sir Francis Drake Society‹. A contemporary of Claude Garamond, Sir Francis Drake lived from 1540 to 1596. He already has many devoted followers and admirers in the graphics industry. Large software companies and type designers in the digital area will welcome Sir Francis Drake as their patron. In 1581 Queen Elizabeth knighted him for his achievements and later he was elected Member of the Parliament.

Let's bring Sir Francis Drake's life back to the minds of those not familiar with his daring deeds. In the 16th century, Francis Drake was a relentless pirate who took hold of everything he desired. Aren't we – living in the 20th century – confronted with similar actions in the field of type design owing to the fact that type designers in all countries suffer from a lack of copyright protection for their work and their property? There are a number of pirates raising the Jolly Roger everywhere, but when ashore they attend large-scale conferences where they claim to devote themselves to the colors of honorable shipping companies.

Something happened in September 1993 in the harbor city of Antwerp. The Association Typographique Internationale had a conference and talked about an ›Anti-Piracy Campaign‹. Some firms had become angry about the illegal copies of their software, a loss of income in the millions. Mac and PC users should buy only original software and no cheap copies. Such font software includes alphabets, which means the creative work of type designers. These designers also feel originals should be sold, and no copies.

Recently, to the other existing copies of my Palatino sold under obscure names, a new poor copy was added, named ›Book Antiqua‹ and sold to a giant software firm. They put their own copyright on the diskettes with ›All rights reserved‹ underneath. What rights are left to the originator? I had no information, no possibility to make corrections, and of course have received not a cent for royalties. Such big software companies should have the best Palatino for their customers and not such a cheap copy.

The firm producing this ›Book Antiqua‹ was a speaker on behalf of the ›Anti-Piracy Campaign‹. This caused me to resign in Antwerp as a founding member of ATypI after 36 years. This organization was established in Lausanne in 1957 by Charles Peignot to internationally protect the creative work of type designers and also of typefounders. Great names had been connected with ATypI in its history – personalities like Beatrice Warde, Stanley Morison, Giovanni Mardersteig, Willem Ovink, Roger Excoffon, Georg Trump, etc.

Even in business there are some rules! You can't steal apples from your neighbor's orchard and sell them as your own product at the market to get money. Even if your neighbor has no fence around his property, it is not allowed, for we are living in a civilized time. Apples are apples and alphabets are alphabets is a simple answer. But we know there are all kinds of apples with different brands and there are also different typefaces – some with names like Palatino and Optima. The situation with typefaces is: They have no real fence by copyright law.

Another example perhaps for the U. S. Copyright Office in Washington, D.C. is this. A picture taken with a cheap camera by an amateur in 1/1000 of a second has at once the backing of the international copyright. But there may be in the future some new legal questions that will arise, by taking from a TV set pictures for commercial use without permission, eventually to manipulate, or by cropping essential parts or changing details electronically. The newest electronic visual systems are producing pictures with a video-printer in seconds. These people don't think about what they are doing with images of a pretty blond or of a famous sports hero.

Nobody would copy a record of Leonard Bernstein's ›West Side Story‹ and sell it under another copyright. Nobody can make a reprint of a work of literature with a new title by changing the author's name.

A typeface is sometimes the result of developments over years – e.g. Optima from 1950 to 1958 – and in the end is the creative work of a designer without any protection against copying.

But a logo done of a few letters of an existing alphabet has the backing of a trademark or copyright like ›expo67‹ for the exhibition in Montreal in Optima. Or take the IBM logo – three letters of Georg Trump's typeface ›City Bold‹. On the other hand, the complete alphabet has no international protection at all. The manipulations of original drawings of artists will become more and more a common

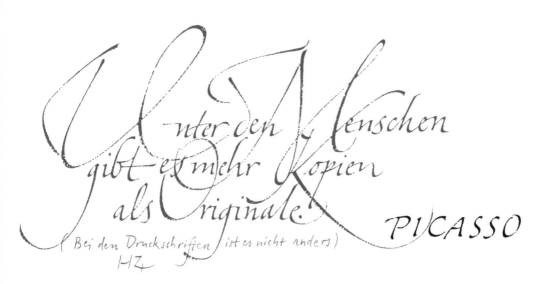

Unter den Menschen gibt es mehr Kopien als Originale. PICASSO

(Bei den Druckschriften ist es nicht anders) HZ

---

procedure, and some will wake up when such people discover that their own work was used or copied to fill the pockets of someone else.

Some contemporaries expect a type designer to work for nothing – as a crusader or pioneer in the battle against illiteracy – with all his simple heart in a social engagement – but in the end to feed big companies. In short: this is making profit with the intellectual property of others.

I doubt that lawyers are helping people in the sad situation of a poor man out of a human feeling for him, working for nothing, paying out of their own pocket the expenses of employees and others. But in the case of a type designer, it is all right to get not a nickel for distribution rights of a creative work. Copyists have no risk in the manufacturing and promotion of a successful typeface. It is so easy under the existing laws to take creative artwork for nothing, without authorization, not mentioning the source. It looks to the user as he buys the development that he is compensating the firm's investment in research and developing.

We have an inflation of alphabets in these days – a lot of new and fresh ideas but also many bad designs. Too many, you may say. But you can be sure the acceptance of some of these creations will be corrected by the market. As in the past, only the good design will stand. Much of this ephemera will soon be forgotten and, no question, nobody will copy those alphabets.

Type reflects trends and developments, like any other artistic activity. They follow fashion streams. This is not so much in text faces, for our eyes are still the same as in Gutenberg's time. But in display type, the design must be attractive enough to catch the attention of the reader. Here is still an interesting opportunity for new ideas.

Today fewer neutral or anonymous alphabets are wanted, but more individual interpretations, some with a pronounced personal hand. In addition, the computer is now entering into creative areas – the sole domain of a designer in the past. With a PC and the possibility of morphing, it is now possible to get new solutions which never existed before. Such developments are welcome and have many positive aspects – as long as they are not getting into the hands of pseudo-designers.

The danger for the future is the endless possibility of manipulating existing alphabets; to sell them as one's own creations. In a few years we will have a complete bastardization. It will be hard to identify what is an original alphabet and what is a modified and miserable botch for the ordinary reader – and yes, even the so-called experts – who don't see the tiny little differences in the small reading sizes«.

(Copyright 1994 by Hermann Zapf. From the ›Bulletin‹ of the Typographers International Association / TIA, February 1994, Flemington / New Jersey).

The sad experience with ›Book Antiqua‹ mentioned in the Francis Drake story was for me a very bitter disappointment, especially since the copy of Palatino roman was done by a former colleague and with whom I had worked for many years in Frankfurt.

But now to a contemporary design called ›Zapfino Script‹, a typeface that entered a new territory in the making of script fonts. The type was developed by using many of the possibilities of digital technology at hand. The new OpenType format has the ability to offer a large variety of letterform solutions.

Zapfino Script

Zapfino Script started as a suggestion by David Siegel. I had previously worked with him in connection with the AMS-Euler typeface project by Prof. Donald E. Knuth for the American Mathematical Society. After completing his studies at the Computer Science Department at Stanford in 1985, David – among other things – worked for the startup company ›Pixar Animation Studios‹, painted Macintoshes for the 1987 Mac Expo (in pink, violet, marble and even wood), and developed typefaces of his own (Tekton, Graphite, and Eaglefeather). In 1992, he founded his own company and wanted to get into the type business.

He wrote me, saying he had a fantastic idea which involved a new kind of typeface that had to have a large number of variations. The idea was to recreate handwriting on the computer. To make it realistic, the joining strokes between the letters would be made by the computer contextually: ›the letters will find each other, as in a true handwritten script‹ and the height of the baseline could vary, as with normal handwriting. His software would add swashes at the beginnings and ends of paragraphs or lines and substitute fancy or special characters in almost any situation.

It looked great. But David wanted to start at once using a calligraphic example I had reproduced in a publication for the Society of Typographic Arts in Chicago. In my opinion, this was the absolute wrong way to go, and I was very worried about it. While I was of course interested in working on a complicated program, I was a little concerned about starting something absolutely new without any technical instructions.

But then I remembered the example of calligraphy in my sketchbook from 1944: the quotation by Hans von Weber. It had already been the model for ›Virtuosa Script‹ in 1947, but the result was a compromise, because of all the restrictions on swashes in a metal typeface. This page from my sketchbook of 1944 now became the inspiration for drawings of ›Zapfino‹, a name given eventually to this new typeface. (See p. 21).

The free and lively writing of this piece established Zapfino's key design features: the marriage of narrow lowercase letters with relatively

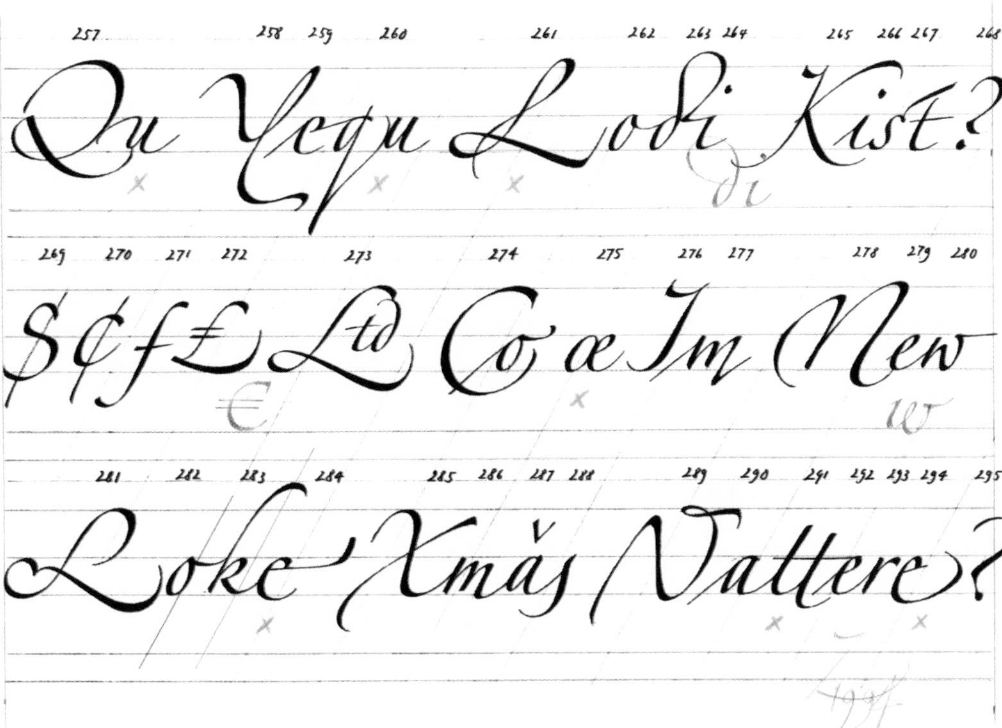

wide letter spacing, swash characters that often overlap the characters in subsequent lines, and different capital letters mixed within text. Only with digital technology could the result I wanted be attained.

David Siegel took on Gino Lee, a designer from Boston, who moved to Palo Alto bursting with enthusiasm to digitize the typeface. It was a pleasure to work with him, and I hardly had to correct his work.

In 1996, after attempting to license the technology to HP and Agfa without any success at the end, our ambitious type-technology project was dropped. Unfortunately, this long-shot program would never have worked as we first intended. The font production cost was just too high, and the economics of the time made it impossible to sell. David turned in 1995 to internet development and wrote ›Creating Killer Websites‹ which turned out to be the top seller for Amazon in 1996. His studio Verso was growing rapidly and so busy with customer work that further development of Zapfino was impossible. In addition, Gino Lee, who now was co-founder and Senior Designer, was busy growing their new company. This unfortunately caused a delay as the type market really suffered during this time while the web design market was just beginning.

With all these ups and downs, the development of Zapfino had been seriously delayed. That was until I plucked up the courage to show the project to Linotype in 1997, who decided they were prepared to complete the project. Linotype first put the whole project into some semblance of order. We eventually agreed on four alphabets, throwing some letters out and adding a few new ones. After that, we had even more to include: 100 ornaments, pen flourishes, calligraphic index characters, etc. Index characters are usually masculine fists, but Zapfino also has elegant ladies' hands. I think the first time such symbols were used in a typeface was when I designed them for the ITC Dingbats.

The basic concept at the start of the Zapfino project in 1993 was the automatic mixing of different letters in the sequence within a word. No letter design should be repeated; up to six variations were available. In the Linotype version of Zapfino, we have only four variants to interchange manually without automating the process. But the very first idea of having a more individual and lively expression in composition was still our focus.

Certainly Zapfino touches the domain of calligraphic letterforms but can never imitate the personal originality of the hand. The accidental irregularities of the writing tool and spontaneous expression of the letter-

forms will always be the calligrapher's special domain; no typeface will ever reach this privilege. (See pp. 128 and 129).

Zapfino signifies the overthrowing of the usual monotony of typography. It ends the repeating structure of letters, as was the normal principle in metal type. This was carried over into photocomposition and to some extent in digital composition. When used with care and creativity, Zapfino effectively adds variety and intermixture to composition.

Originally I thought Zapfino would be used in relatively small sizes for personal ephemera. After the initial release of the four Zapfino designs in 1998, we noticed how it was being used in huge dimensions for outdoor advertising. The digital technique allows enlargements in proportions that could never be done by the former photocomposition process, and now the outlines are absolutely sharp no matter what the size. These new considerations led to the decision to redesign Zapfino in some details and to add new letters to cover the possibilities I had in mind. So ›Zapfino Extra‹ was developed in connection with the new OpenType format that has no limitations on the number of characters that can be in a font. The dream of a type designer.

After Apple licensed the rights to use and expand Zapfino, further augmentations were discussed at a meeting on September 10, 2001, with Steve Jobs and Peter Lofting. (This was one day before the terrible events on September 11, which changed the way of life worldwide).

To the final list of characters that would be in Zapfino Extra, we decided to add ligatures of capital letters for titles and abbreviations, special jubilee figures, lowercase characters with up-strokes to be used at the beginning of words, small caps, ordinal numbers, and mathematical signs, etc. These would complete the existing set of letterforms. Already we had so-called ›hyper-flourishes‹, which are big swashes running over two text lines. We also added 100 ornament designs, some of them very fancy looking. (See p. 126).

The digitization of Zapfino Extra was done by Akira Kobayashi (born 1960 in Japan). He is an expert in the handling of a Macintosh. It was an ideal collaboration that often reminded me of my time with my punch-cutter August Rosenberger at the former D. Stempel AG typefoundry in Frankfurt.

Zapfino Extra got a bold version called ›Zapfino Forte‹, a welcome addition that can be used to emphasize product names or accentuate company names within a running text page. This bold version has a reduced number of characters, and includes only those truly needed for emphasis within text lines.

Zapfino Ink

And there is also a new design called ›Zapfino Ink‹. The letters in this alphabet have the appearance of flowing ink within their forms, and may be used for very personal messages and for writing addresses. My first attempts with an ink effect go back to the very beginning of the Zapfino development. I did experiments for forgery-safe documents and signatures in 1993, which were done with screened halftones to get different degrees of shading. But the technical possibilities at that time were very limited by computer space. The idea was finally realized in Zapfino Ink. I must confess that by the end, the Zapfino adventure was the most complicated task I ever accomplished in my whole career as a type designer during all these many years.

The next work was another big project with Akira Kobayashi. It was my new digital version of Optima called ›Optima nova‹, released by Linotype GmbH in the year 2003. It is a completely redesigned Optima for perfect digital performance. For instance, the old Optima had no real italic but only an obliqued (or slanted) roman. But the requirements for metal Linotype fonts allowed an oblique of only 12 degrees. The newly designed Optima nova Italic has a slant of 15 degrees. Optima nova is easy to identify by its real italic that has a nice new f design, contrary to the old amputated f which was a holdover from the age of lead. Look also at the e, g, and lowercase l for identifying characteristics, just to mention a few of the new shapes in the italic version. And the former duck beak upstroke of the figure 1 (like Donald Duck) has been changed to a cheeky new design in the manner of Pinocchio's nose. Optima nova also has new designed oldstyle figures, small caps, italic small caps and a condensed design.

Beide Optima Alphabete sind gut zu unterscheiden, besonders in den Buchstaben e, f und g bei der Optima nova Italic und gegenüber der schräg gestellten Antiqua der alten Optima.

It is easy to identify the two versions of Optima, for Optima nova Italic differs greatly from the old slanted Roman of the original Optima. The new Italic forms of the e, f and g are especially notable.

In total, Optima nova consists of 20 alphabets. It even includes the freshly designed ›Optima Titling‹, an all-caps design with several very unusual ligatures and letter combinations, bringing the total number of characters in Optima nova Titling to 84. A characteristic design element in Optima Titling is the use of rounded corners on the letterforms, an idea I had used in former calligraphic sculptures in aluminum. (See p. 84).

The cover of the Optima nova type specimen shows both sides of the 1,000 lire banknote on which the first sketches of the letterforms were done on October 3, 1950. I had no paper available to make sketches from inscriptions in the Santa Croce Church in Florence, so I used a bank note instead. (See p. 33). The type specimen includes Optima nova Titling and several illustrations of Optima in use around the world. There is a picture showing the inscriptions of the 58,000 names on the Vietnam Veterans Memorial in Washington D.C. The samples of Optima in use also include postal stamps and street signs in Nancy/France.

Another bigger project with Akira Kobayashi was the Linotype Platinum Collection of the ›Palatino Family‹. (See p. 133). This new release includes redesigns of the various Palatino nova alphabets, an improved design of the Michelangelo, the Greek Phidias, Sistina capitals, Aldus Book, Palatino Greek and Palatino Cyrillic. The cover of the type specimen for the Palatino type family shows a portrait of the name patron, the writing master Giovanbattista Palatino. Inside there are earlier examples showing the types in use; including the first printing of Palatino in the 1956 annual report from the Standard Oil Company in New Jersey, and Aldus used in ›Gesammelte Werke von Thomas Mann‹ (the collected works in 12 volumes from S. Fischer Verlag in Frankfurt/Germany). A quotation by Plato about the importance of letters composed in Palatino Greek is also shown on a page.

В. Лазурский

›Palatino Cyrillic‹ is a new alphabet that has been added to this collection. I had previously studied Cyrillic letterforms in 1960 in order to do the calligraphy for the Russian text in ›The Preamble of the Charter of the United Nations‹. At that time, I started a correspondence with Prof. Wadim Wladomirowitsch Lazursky, a type designer in Moscow. Unsuspecting, I sent him a few Cyrillic letters to get his opinion about how I would write them with a broad-edged pen. This was quite naive on my part, as I learned years later after I became personally acquainted with him in Prague. He told me we had been really lucky the letters were not opened by the Soviet censors, for they would have jumped to the conclusion that the strange combination of a few letters could only be a secret message from the bad capitalist West. Remarkable in contrast, Lazursky's letters to me were opened by the German authorities.

Microsoft Corp. Inc.

In 1995 I was again involved with Cyrillic and intensively studied the letterforms designed since the period of Czar Peter the Great. But this time, I examined not only Russian letterforms, but also those for people in the Caucasus and nearby countries who use Cyrillic for their languages. It was the wish of Bill Gates of the Microsoft Corporation Inc. to expand Palatino to cover the languages of all countries with letterforms that are based on the Latin, Greek, or Cyrillic alphabets, including Vietnamese. At the end of this mighty job, the OpenType version of Palatino had 1,218 characters each in the normal, bold, italic and bold italic fonts, for a total of 4,872 letters. To celebrate this super typographic event, Microsoft printed four big posters in 1997 showing all the glyphs. (Reproduced in ›The Fine Art of Letters: The Work of Hermann Zapf‹, Grolier Club, New York 2000, page 77). Unfortunately Wadim Lazursky could not witness the process or the completion of the Palatino Cyrillic type design, for he passed away in Moscow on July 4, 1993, at the age of 84. But Palatino Cyrillic was celebrated by the Academy of Graphic Design in Moscow in 1996, which means it must have looked pretty good to Russian eyes.

Palatino Sans

But this is not quite the end of the Palatino story. While working on the new digital version of Palatino, Otmar Hoefer from Linotype GmbH suggested a sans serif be added to the Palatino Roman family. This typeface, called ›Palatino Sans‹ is a newly designed sans serif with a human touch; it was deliberately drawn quite differently from most sans serif

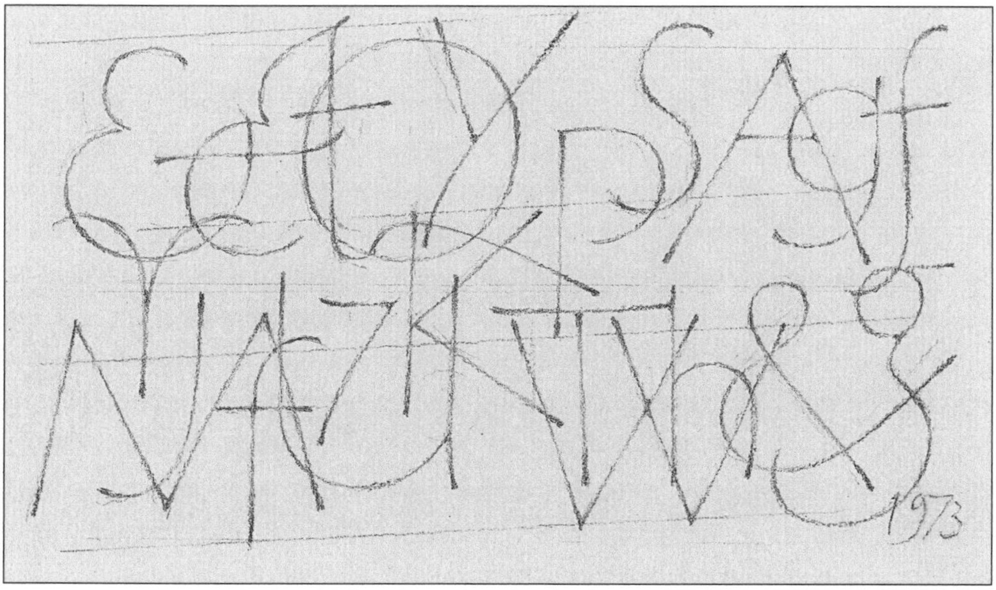

types that are constructed with the technical exactness of ruler-drawn straight lines. There is also a second sans serif alphabet with a series of alternate characters named ›Palatino Sans Informal‹.

It was not a big problem for me to make the drawings, for I had already tried a similar theme for a more personal sans serif several years ago; it was intended to be produced for photocomposition. In 1973, I showed the sans serif project to the Stempel typefoundry in Frankfurt, but unfortunately my idea did not meet with enthusiasm. At that time, everything was completely dominated by the dry ›Helvetica‹. So now, for the new Linotype Palatino Sans, I had only to make a redesign of my old softer looking drawings. (See pp. 135 and 137).

Palatino Arabic

A new supplement to ›Palatino nova‹ is a digital redesign of the former ›Al-ahram Arabic‹, which was originally produced as a metal type. This digital redesign was done together with Nadine Chahine of Beirut from 2005 to 2006, enlarged with Urdu and Persian letters. The weight of the new ›Palatino Arabic‹ is well balanced with the Palatino nova for mixing both alphabets in bilingual documents.

The 50-year-old design concept of Palatino has proved its validity, for her letters have not been seen as modish interpretations, nor as historic expressions of passed epochs. We do not erect Renaissance palaces or build Baroque churches anymore. We are living in a totally changed society where the individual aspires to create his own specific expression. Today, type design is industrial design, and type is integrated in the digital surroundings of our present time.

The work of a type designer needs more care and precision compared with other design disciplines. A badly designed letter within an alphabet might be used million of times and can't be corrected as soon as it is fixed. Scarely any other creative activity has such worldwide dissemination.

Just a couple of examples are Palatino and Optima in their use on insignificant stamps. Both type faces can be found in nearly every country on earth, from Azerbaijan to Singapore, from America to Vietnam, from the Fiji Islands to Germany. Of the ›Americana‹ collection of the United States alone more than 72 million were printed in the 1980s. The international flag stamps of the United Nations should also be mentioned, again with ›Optima Roman‹.

The time of compromises for composition in rigid metal type is gone. In the past ten years, the digital generation of text has brought many advantages. Kerned letters, hung punctuation, and letters extending into margins are easily possible, even at the smallest type sizes. Today a multitude of type sizes are available, compared to the rigid standard sizes in metal. Special characters are now a common component of fonts, and they are often designed in the same style as the text face, instead of plugging in generic substitutes. Letterforms are no longer squeezed into a unit system as was necessary for the Monotype typesetting systems or for photocomposition. Corrections to text composition can be made with much less effort. And last, but not least, those who like the ›bite impression‹ of letterpress printing in contrast to the ›kiss impression‹ of offset printing can have the effect of type and images penetrating the surface of the paper by using photo-polymer plates for printing.

The printed letter – or a well-designed book – is something very unique compared to the fleeting resolution of a screen and quick access on the internet. A book offers a happy feeling in the hands of the reader and is quite different from an abstract electronic presentation of text.

In a few years, books printed by the classic letterpress technique will receive a new esteem. Today they are sometimes disregarded as products of a past time compared to what can be done with modern methods of composition and printing. But we should not forget they are examples of our cultural heritage and should not be forgotten, for they are still the standards for all new achievements. Today's easy digital input of text and the perfect digital resolution of letterforms may seem to dim the highlights of fine book production. But such books are still expressions of creative activities, and their execution often requires hard work. Remember the compositor of the past, who placed type in the composing stick with care and patience, one letter at a time. Perhaps that compositor was more closely connected to his work than the user of a computer today. We know in the meantime the many inadequacies and the limitation of Gutenberg's methods, but we approach them by improving our works with the present digital opportunities. There are no limits for individual designs. Only the technical requirements have changed.

* * *

At the end, my thanks to my wife for all her critical support,
her patience and her understanding for my work and ideas in all the many years
of my professional life which we have shared together.

Frontispiece (p. 4) – Watercolor painted April 1945 in a military hospital at Tübingen while a French prisoner of war. It was hidden by friends because of my possible transfer to quarantine at Nagold in the Black Forest. Pictured here at actual size. A description of the individual elements may be found on page 18.

5 – ›San Francisco Examiner‹. The edition dated November 11, 1918 reporting ›Peace on earth. Germany surrenders‹.

6 – 1 Billion Marks. Reduced copy of the Reichsbank note from November 5, 1923 (original size 143 x 85 mm). It is unimaginable that, at the end of the inflation period, a billion marks were means of payment. That is 1,000 million. The assessed value of a dollar amounted to 4.2 billion reichsmarks. In mid-November 1923, the reichsmark was replaced by the new rentenmark. 1 billion reichsmarks became 1 rentenmark. This ended the inflation.

7 – Nuremberg Castle. Drawn from memory while home from school; I was seven years old, and the drawing does not completely correspond with reality. Particularly interesting are the decorated initials, which also appear in a poem by Joseph von Eichendorff from the year 1932.

8 – Electrical Experiment Kit. Cover and title page of the instruction book, September/October 1933. On the little cover tab is a reference to the famous 1789 bioelectrical experiment with electrical current and a frog thigh by Luigi Galvani (1737–1798). In the design for the title page, a double L ligature is used that would reappear 60 years later in ›Optima nova Titling‹. (See p. 131).

12 – ›Haus zum Fürsteneck‹ in Frankfurt am Main. Wash drawing from 1938. View from Garküchenplatz on the Fürsteneck in the Fahrgasse. On the left are the old grain scales from 1719, which were restored at considerable expense in 1938. Six years later, they were destroyed during an air raid on Frankfurt's historic district.

14 – ›Alkor Musical Notation‹. Designed in 1939 for the Bärenreiter music publisher in Kassel-Wilhemshöhe as a two-color typeface for musical notation. Since the staves were printed in red, simple scores could be set with a linecasting typesetter. When the Bärenreiter printing house was destroyed in March 1945, the matrices and composing machines were annihilated as well.

15 – ›Musica presto‹. The cursive musical notation typeface with this provisory name was scheduled to be produced in 1943 by C. E. Röder in Leipzig as an experiment. However, everything was lost during an air raid in December 1943. The first calligraphic trials for the design were made during my time at Paul Koch's ›Haus zum Fürsteneck‹ in Frankfurt in 1938. The image is of a score by Heinrich Spitta from my war sketchbook done in 1941. Additionally there is a comparison with notes from the score of Ludwig van Beethoven's Ninth Symphony, 1825.

16 – ›Gilgengart‹. Original drawings of Gilgengart Fraktur in 48 point for the punchcutter August Rosenberger, dated March 19, 1939. Also shown are variants for the capital D.

After Fraktur type was banned in 1941, D. Stempel AG halted the casting of Gilgengart. It was the last Fraktur type to be cut by a type foundry in Germany.

19 – Henry W. Longfellow ›Nuremberg‹. Two watercolors from my calligraphic manuscript ›Nuremberg‹, a poem by Henry W. Longfellow, showing the famous fountain at Hauptmarkt and the Albrecht Dürer house. The volume has 24 watercolors, including the title page, which were each 6.5 x 7 cm. (Dated August 8, 1938).

21 – Hans von Weber. Calligraphy from ›Gedanken und Skizzen 1942–1955‹, shown at original size. Written with a Sommerville copperplate pen and watercolor ink in Bordeaux, 1944. (The lowercase letters have a height of 1.5 mm). The text shows the utilization of various upper and lowercase letters, as well as swashes that extend beyond the lines, like those that would be used in the digital ›Zapfino‹ script 50 years later.
Translation: »One may well hesitate before deciding whether to devote one's life to books or to women. Can you, when she has her whims, put a woman back into the bookcase? And what if a book, without asking your leave, were to go out of your library and onto another's bookshelf? Can a book demand that you read no other volume but devote yourself to its pages – despite your own wish to read another – or just as you are ready for bed (or intending simply to do nothing)? Will soups be over-salted by books? Can books pout or sulk? Or play the piano? Books, however, still have one blessed deficiency: they cannot kiss!«

23 – ›Palatino Italic‹. Master artwork in 36 point for the punchcutter August Rosenberger. Dated June 1939 – October 1951. Since it was made for handsetting, the design is narrower than the Palatino Italic that was developed for the Linotype machine, whose characters had widths identical to their Roman counterparts. For comparison, trial proofs from the punchcutter are glued above the letter drawings. Originally called ›Medici Kursiv‹, the name of the typeface was later changed.

24 – ›Pen and Graver‹. This page shows decorated uppercase Fraktur letters. The book contained 26 lettering panels, of which eight depicted white letters on a black background. Each panel is 21 x 11.5 cm. The master artwork for each panel was drawn for August Rosenberger at actual size. These were photographically transferred onto lead plates, which he then engraved. An appendix summarized the evolution of writing, from the Greek alphabet to the German Current handwriting style.

27 – Photo of August Rosenberger. A picture taken together with August Rosenberger in his small workshop in the D. Stempel AG type foundry in Frankfurt am Main. The photograph was made during a visit by Valter Falk from Stockholm. In the background are two pages from ›Pen and Graver‹. We both look quite melancholy here; perhaps we had just gotten into trouble with the foundry managers again.

31 (top) – ›Melior Roman‹. Design for the ›Linotype Melior‹ uppercase, with an attached test line printed at 12 point, dated May 28, 1952. The Melior Roman, Melior Bold, and Melior Italic are drawn on graph paper to show that the same characters in each version are of the same width. At the lower right, two Linotype matrices are reproduced.

(The image on p. 115 shows a revision of the hot metal Melior for the Linofilm phototypesetting machine from 1966).

31 (bottom) – ›Virtuosa I & II‹. A sketch with alternatives for the uppercase as well as 11 possibilities for the ampersand. Dated December 9, 1950. The fantasies of the designer

were badly reduced during the production of the typeface. Unfortunately, typefaces cast for handsetting could not offer many letter variants, since space in the type case drawers was limited. (Compare with the image on p. 111).

32 – Santa Croce, Florence. Sketches from the marble letters on the graves of Florentine families, from the floor inside Santa Croce. These acted as the stimulus for the later ›Optima Roman‹. In some cases, the letters maintain the hint of serifs, but they keep the rhythm of the older letters that they were modeled on.

33 – 1,000 Lire note. Front and back of a 1,000 Lire banknote, on which sketches were made in 1950 for the serif-less Roman that would later be named ›Optima Roman‹. On the front are sketches of the inlaid letters from the floor at Santa Croce. The back depicts sketches that were already intended to lead to a proper typeface; these were made later in the hotel room, and were named ›Florentina‹ and ›Firenze‹. (In my opinion, my original names were much better than the absolutist-sounding name ›Optima‹, which was later decided upon by the D. Stempel AG type foundry and Linotype GmbH).

35 – ›Manuale Typographicum‹. Significantly reduced page from the 1954 edition. (Original size 19.5 x 10.5 cm). Emery Walker was a contemporary of William Morris who lived from 1851–1933. The Manuale was printed in 16 languages on copperplate printing paper at the D. Stempel AG internal printing office in Frankfurt am Main.

The page numbers were blind-stamped into the paper. The M.I.T. Press in Cambridge, Massachusetts, produced an English-language reprint of the text samples at original size in 1970 via offset printing. The text is from Emery Walker's preface to the catalogue of the Arts and Crafts Exhibition Society, London 1888.

38 – ›Al-ahram Arabic‹. First text sample tests with Arabic. Quote from Johann Wolfgang von Goethe's ›West-östlicher Divan‹. In German: »An Gutenberg. Unserm Meister, geh! Verpfände / Dich, o Büchlein, traulich froh / Hier am Anfang, hier am Ende / Östlich, westlich, A und Ω«. (»To Gutenberg. Grave and joyous little book, / give obeisance to thy Master. / Begin at dawn and end at sunset, / from the Alpha to Omega«).

40 – Teaching at RIT. A diagram drawn from the blackboard representing the teaching method. It proceeds from a starting point, to which one can always come back in order to begin again if no progress has been achieved. Its intention was to recreate courage again and again.

42 – Plato ›Philebos 51c‹. The text is an analysis of the construction of Greek letters and their geometric proportions. Excerpt from a lettering panel made with the sgraffito technique; oil and tempera paint on a prepared ground. (Size of the panel: 40 x 60 cm). The calligraphic Greek has scores of ligatures and variants. (A complete image may be found in ›Hermann Zapf and his design philosophy‹, Society of Typographic Arts, Chicago 1987, p. 37).

45 – ›Typographic Variations‹. Printed on copperplate paper. The margins and page numbers are blind-stamped into the paper, and many of the typographic examples were tipped in. The images show the title ›American Theater‹ for the Gutenberg Book Guild in Frankfurt, a series of plays from various countries. Title pages combined with tables

of contents were novel. The second example is a title page for the poetry volume ›Les Fleurs du Mal‹ by Charles Baudelaire. The style of the calligraphic lines and the ornament makes them seem as though they were drawn with lipstick.

48 – Program IBM 1130. Extract from the draft for the programming of the computer with help from the paper tape that was common at the time. (Complete image shown in ›ABC-XYZapf‹. Wynkyn de Worde Society, London 1989, p. 58). The program succeeded in finding a relatively simple solution for optically spacing uppercase letters, which worked perfectly, even in small point sizes. In handsetting, machine typesetting, and photo typesetting, this was always a very cumbersome work.

51 – ›Orbis Typographicus‹. Page set in ›Perikles‹, a typeface designed by Robert Foster for the American Type Founders Inc. (ATF). The text is a double-anagram (by Franz Pahnem). The vignette was cut in lead by August Rosenberger.

55 (top) – ›Marconi and Aurelia Roman & Italic‹. Two digital alphabets developed for Dr. Ing. Rudolf Hell GmbH in Kiel. Drawings for Marconi were 10 cm. The project was started in 1973. It was new design territory for all of us. The alphabet went into production in 1976. The second example shows letters for Aurelia Roman of 1981.

55 (bottom) – Vietnam Veterans Memorial, Washington D.C. Stone rubbing from one of the 58,200-plus names on the memorial's black granite. These can be made per request by volunteer helpers. (The letters are 14 mm high).

The use of ›Optima Roman‹ was suggested to the architect Maya Lin by Julian Waters in Washington, who became my successor in alphabet design at Rochester Institute of Technology in 1988.

58 – ›Sequoyah Syllabary‹. The revision of this syllabary, made by the Cherokee Indians during the 19th century, was particularly difficult. The 85 symbols invented by Chief Sequoyah were rather uncommon and unsystematic. My preliminary work began with several studies in libraries and archives, and is from the year 1977.

62 – Rudolf Koch. (Born in Nuremberg in 1876; died in Frankfurt in 1934). The text is an entry from him in a 1932 guestbook. Example of a calligraphic Fraktur from the sketchbook ›Thoughts and Sketches 1941/42‹ dated October 1, 1941, in Weimar.

Translation: »Lettermaking in every form gives me the purest and greatest pleasure and on numberless occasions in my life it has been to me what a song is to the singer, a painting to the painter, a shout to the joyous, and a sigh to the afflicted – to me it is the happiest and most perfect expression of my life.«

64 – ›AMS Euler‹. This design was the result of a project to create a comprehensive mathematical typeface family for Stanford University and the American Mathematical Society (AMS) in Providence, Rhode Island. The instigation came from Prof. Donald E. Knuth, Department of Computer Science, Stanford University. The masters for digitization were precise contour drawings that had been made with an extra fine ballpoint, from which sample letters, mathematical symbols, special characters, numerators, etc. could be made in 10 point, 9 point, and even smaller sizes, in order to submit them to mathematicians for evaluation.

70 – ›Zapf Essentials‹. A small selection from the 372 Essentials symbols. Published by Linotype in 2004 as an extension of ›Zapf Dingbats‹, which was produced by the International Typeface Corporation, New York, in 1977. After 25 years, symbols for new technologies such as mobile phones, e-mail, and fax machines were added.

73 – Pablo Picasso quote. »Regarding people, there are more copies than originals«. Text from my New Year's card, 1994. Given my experience with the copy of Palatino and my resignation from ATypI, the ›Association Typographique Internationale‹, in Antwerp in 1993, I penciled in the following addition: (… with typefaces it is not different).

75 – ›Zapfino Extra‹. Some of the new ligatures and ampersands for the expanded Zapfino from 1998. The 2005 type specimen shows a complete overview of all letters and extra characters, including the 100 ornaments.

The Zapfino Extra CD-ROM offers thorough tips for accessing and using the desired characters, i. e. the so-called ›hyper-flourishes‹. The addition of up-strokes for certain letters is also explained; this was something new for a script face – it helps bring out the handwritten nature even more.

The OpenType version of ›Zapfino Extra‹ is fitted with contextual features. These allow the alternate characters to appear automatically onscreen while one is typing.

The CD-ROM also includes the 16-minute Hallmark film from 1967.

77 – ›Zapfino Hyper-flourishes‹. Digital technology allows for letters to overlap, and even for letters to cross over into other lines. Who would have ever thought that such artwork could be made on a computer? (Compare with the image on p. 127).

78 – ›Zapfino Ink‹. A few letters to show the effect of ink flow, just as they would appear if written with a pen. Zapfino Ink's letters are suited for applications where a handwritten appearance is desired. This effect is strengthened when the text is printed blue.

79 – ›Optima / Optima nova‹. Comparison of the differences between the old Optima Roman and Optima nova. Particularly noticeable changes are the number 1, and the Optima nova Italic letters e, f, g, and l. (From Linotype's Optima nova type specimen, 2004).

81 – ›Palatino Sans‹. Early sketches for a sans serif Roman photo typeface from 1973. The concept was to give the letters a napped contour, in order to clearly differentiate them from other sans serifs. The open P, typical of all Palatino alphabets, is already visible in this sketch, and was included in the digital typeface 30 years later.

84 – ›Hora fugit – Carpe diem‹ (time flies – seize the day). This drawing was the guide for cutting the design in aluminium. The resulting sculpture represented a very early use of laser technology and was produced by John Borell of Steel Art, Inc., Boston, 1982.

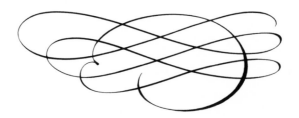

* Beatrix von Kleve. Copy of an illuminated page from the ›Chronik von Kleve‹. (Bavarian State Library, Munich. Cod. gall. 19). An exercise on parchment to study the techniques used by Flemish scribes and illuminators; I carried it out following Edward Johnston's maxim to learn from the old masters.

The Flemish manuscript was executed around 1450, the same time that Johannes Gutenberg printed the 42-line Bible in Mainz using his invention of movable type. In former times, monks wrote each page of a book by hand. Gutenberg's invention more than 500 years ago had an big impact similar to the replacement of metal type by photo-typesetting and digital technologies in our time.

ILLUSTRATIONS

Thomas J. Cobden-Sanderson. Quotation from his essay ›The ideal book or book beautiful‹, printed by the Doves Press in 1900. Shown in a rhythmic arrangement combining calligraphic text together with typeset lines of ›Palatino nova‹ and ›Palatino Sans Informal‹.

Bibliography: Morton Goldscholl: ›Typography-USA‹. New York, 1959. – Douglas C. McMurtie: ›The book. The story of printing and bookmaking‹. New York, London, Toronto, 1950. – Alexander S. Lawson: ›Anatomy of a typeface‹. Boston, 1990. – Donald E. Knuth: »Lessons I learned from Metafont«. In ›Digital typography‹. CSLI Publications, Stanford / California 1999, p. 315. (Previously published in ›Visible Language‹, XIX, Cleveland / Ohio, 1985, p. 35).

Thomas James Cobden-Sanderson (1840–1922) founded the Doves Press in Hammersmith, near London, together with Emery Walker in 1900. This was four years after the end of Willaim Morris's Kelmscott Press. Contrary to Morris's decorative editions, the books from the Doves Press had no ornaments, just pure typography. However, a few editions did include calligraphic initials done by Edward Johnston. The Doves Press also established its own bindery.

This calligraphic example, with text from Cobden-Sanderson, was originally made in 1960 for the students in my class at the Carnegie Institute of Technology in Pittsburgh. It was printed in a limited edition on Japanese paper.

Typography, like the other arts,
is characterized by disciplines
and freedoms.
Typography was born out of the mood
to communicate.
It is a form
that expresses
something other
than itself.

Morton Goldsholl

The whole duty of Typography, as of Calligraphy, is to communicate to the imagination, without loss by the way, the thought or image intended to be communicated by the Author.

THOMAS JAMES COBDEN-SANDERSON

We use the letters of our alphabet
every day
with the utmost ease
and unconcern,
taking them
almost as much
for granted
as the air we breathe.
We do not realize
that each
of these letters
is at our service
today only
as the result of a long
and laboriously slow process
of evolution in the age-old art
of writing.

Douglas C. McMurtrie

The computer
is the most advanced
typographic product
yet to appear;
it would seem
to be the
culmination of
almost five
and a half centuries
of progress
in the transfer
of the scribal hands
to the printed page.

Alexander S. Lawson

Computer programming requires more attention
to detail than anything else that human beings have ever done.
Moreover, the problems of letterform design are extremely subtle,
much more complex than most people think,
because our machines and our eyes interact with the shapes in complicated ways.
I am convinced that digital alphabet design
is an extremely challenging problem, and it is significant enough
to deserve the attention of our best scientific minds
and our best artistic skills and sensitives.

Donald E. Knuth

Electrical experiment kit. Page from the instruction book, written in a German school hand, shown reduced by 16 percent. The book had 76 total pages; I began it on September 11, 1933, in Nuremberg. This page described an attempt to create static electricity with a playing card, as well as instructions on building a radio whose antenna runs through the window without causing any damage.

I had no conception of page layout, but paper had to be saved. The texts were taken in part from trade magazines, and also from published works that I rewrote so that they could be replicated with the primitive possibilities of the tool kit. By July 1932, I had already exchanged letters with the technical editor of ›Europa Funk‹ magazine in Munich; I was just 14 years old.

›The electrical experiment kit in a shoebox‹.
The wire connection idea using a snap-fastener on a thread reel can be seen in the photograph toward the right.

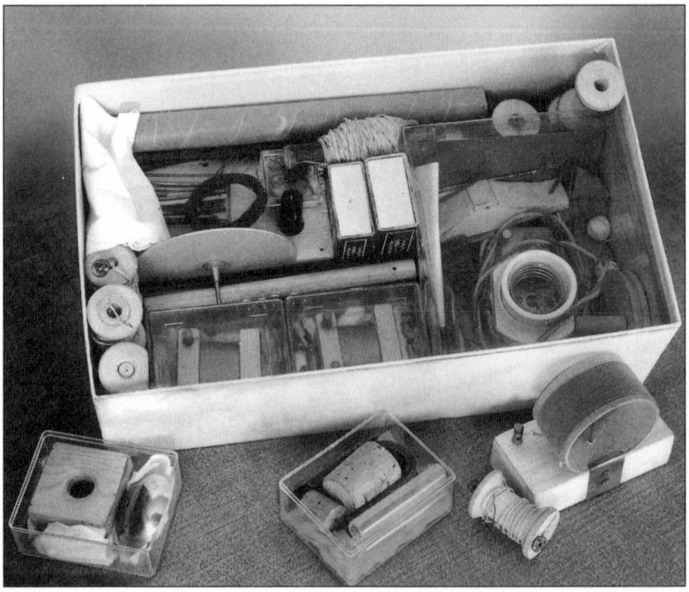

Elektrische Grundversuche:

V. 13. Wir erwärmen das Kartenblatt über dem Ofen ohne es zu versengen, legt es rasch auf den Tisch u. mit einem Wollappen kurz reiben u. dann nähern wir dasselbe den Holundermarkkügelchen usw. Zu unserer Überraschung werden alle diese Dinge angezogen. In der Karte ist durch Reiben eine Kraft erweckt worden, die alle Körper anzieht, also eher der Schwerkraft der Erde gleicht, als dem Magnetismus, der ja nur auf Eisen, Stahl u. Nickel wirkt.

Radio:

N. 1 a

V. 96. Wer in der Nähe einer Rundfunkstation ist, kann diese mit dem einfachen Apparat hören, wenn er die Vorrichtung abstimmbar macht u. Antennen anbringt. Abb. 73. Zur Abstimmung dient der Kondensator, der aus einer etwa dreimal so großen Kupferplatte u. einer gleichgroßen Zinkplatte besteht, von

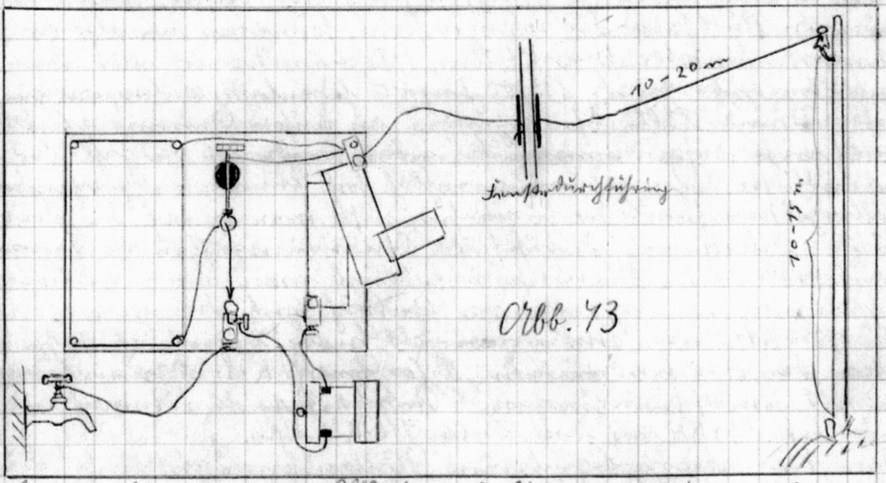

Abb. 73

denen die obere am Schlot gedreht werden kann. Die untere Platte darf von der oberen nirgends berührt werden u. ist darum mit einem Blatt paraffinierten Papiers umwickelt. Die annähernde Abstimmung ist durch die Wahl der Windungszahlen der Spule zu treffen, der Kondensator dient zur Feinabstimmung. Als Antenne verwendet man etwa 10-20 m isolierten Kupferdraht, der zu einer Isolierglocke führt, dieselbe ist auf einer etwa 10-15 m langen Stange isoliert befestigt. Damit man durch Fensterrahmen keine Löcher usw. bohren muß, beklebt man beiderseits eine Fensterscheibe mit einer Staniolscheibe. (Durchmesser zirka 5 cm). An der einen Scheibe führt der Antennendraht, an der anderen der Apparatanschlußdraht.

Wellenlänge u. Kilo-Hertz

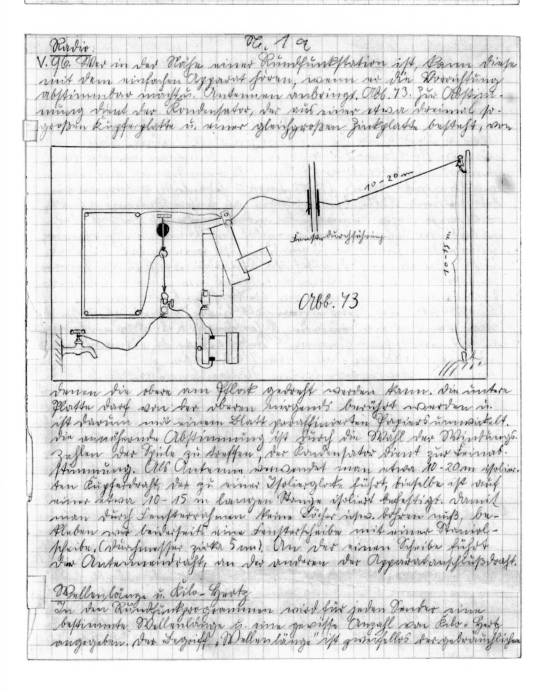

In den Rundfunkprogrammen wird für jeden Sender eine bestimmte Wellenlänge u. eine gewisse Anzahl von Kilo-Hertz angegeben. Der Begriff „Wellenlänge" ist zweifellos der gebräuchliche

Friedrich Hebbel, ›Das Kind‹ (The Child). The poem's verses as paper cuts. (Manuscript HZ No. 5, dated April 9, 1936). The problem was that all of the letters had to be connected in order to prevent their falling apart. Preliminary designs for the best arrangements were therefore necessary. All examples shown are unfortunately greatly reduced in size. My Hebbel manuscript work was still under the strong influence of Rudolf Koch, and inspired by his publication ›The type foundry in silhouettes‹, Offenbach, 1918.

I undertook a similar trial of patience during the war with a text by Gotthold Ephraim Lessing, this time with gold paper. (›Gedanken und Skizzen‹, Thoughts and Sketches, 1941).

Reproduced below is the title page from Rudolf Koch's instruction book, which I used to teach myself to write with a broad-edged pen in 1935.

Das
Schreiben
als Kunstfertigkeit

Eine ausführliche Anleitung zur Erlernung
der für den Beruf des Schreibers
notwendigen Schriftarten
von
Rudolf Koch

3. Auflage
mit einem Anhang von Martin Hermersdorf

Verlag des Deutschen Buchgewerbevereins Leipzig

Das Kind
von Friedrich Hebbel
1813–1863

+

Die Mutter lag im Totenschrein,
zum letztemal geschmückt.
Da spielt das kleine Kind herein,
das staunend sie erblickt.

Die Blumenkron im blonden Haar
gefällt ihm gar zu sehr,
die Busenblumen bunt u. klar
zum Strauß gereiht, noch mehr.

Und sanft u. schmeichelnd ruft es aus:
Du liebe Mutter gib
mir eine Blum aus deinem Strauß,
ich hab dich auch so lieb.

Und als die Mutter es nicht tut,
da denkt das Kind für sich:
sie schläft, doch wenn sie ausgeruht,
so tut sie's sicherlich.

Schleicht fort, so leis es immer kann,
und schließt die Türe sacht
und lauscht von Zeit zu Zeit daran,
ob Mutter noch nicht wacht.

Zum 2. Todestage Rudolf Kochs
am 9. April MDCCCCXXXVI

A retouch done as an apprentice. This is one of the few retouches that I did in 1937, during my four years as an apprentice in the firm of Karl Ulrich & Co in Nuremberg. Most of my time was spent retouching lettering. The illustration on page 101 is slightly reduced.

Very few people know what the work of a retoucher before the war involved, or how it was done. An artistic-handicraft profession, it required a great deal of care. For the gradients on the photographs, an extremely fine airbrush – an aerograph – was used. All other artwork had to be made with a pointed brush and special retouching colors. Straight lines were made with a brush and a ruler. A retoucher could give a machine, for example, an extra robust appearance for a sales brochure. He could make a person's face look much younger, or correct wrinkles much better than an expensive cream by Helena Rubinstein could ever do. All these time-consuming tasks can be completed today much more quickly using digital programs; the retoucher's profession does not exist anymore.

An additional picture on this page compares a photograph before and after retouching.

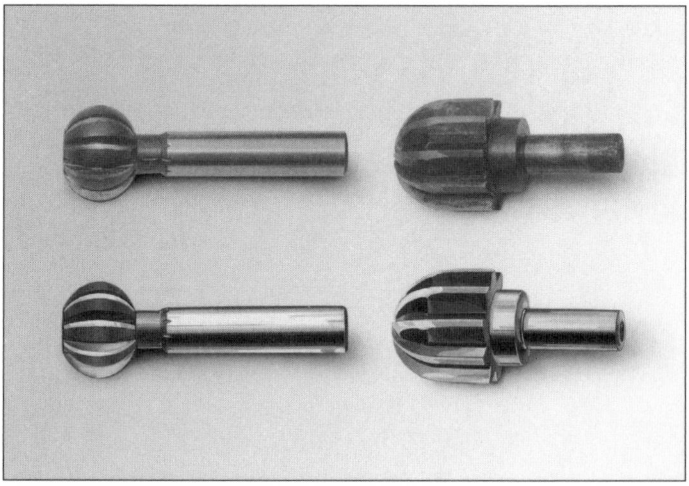

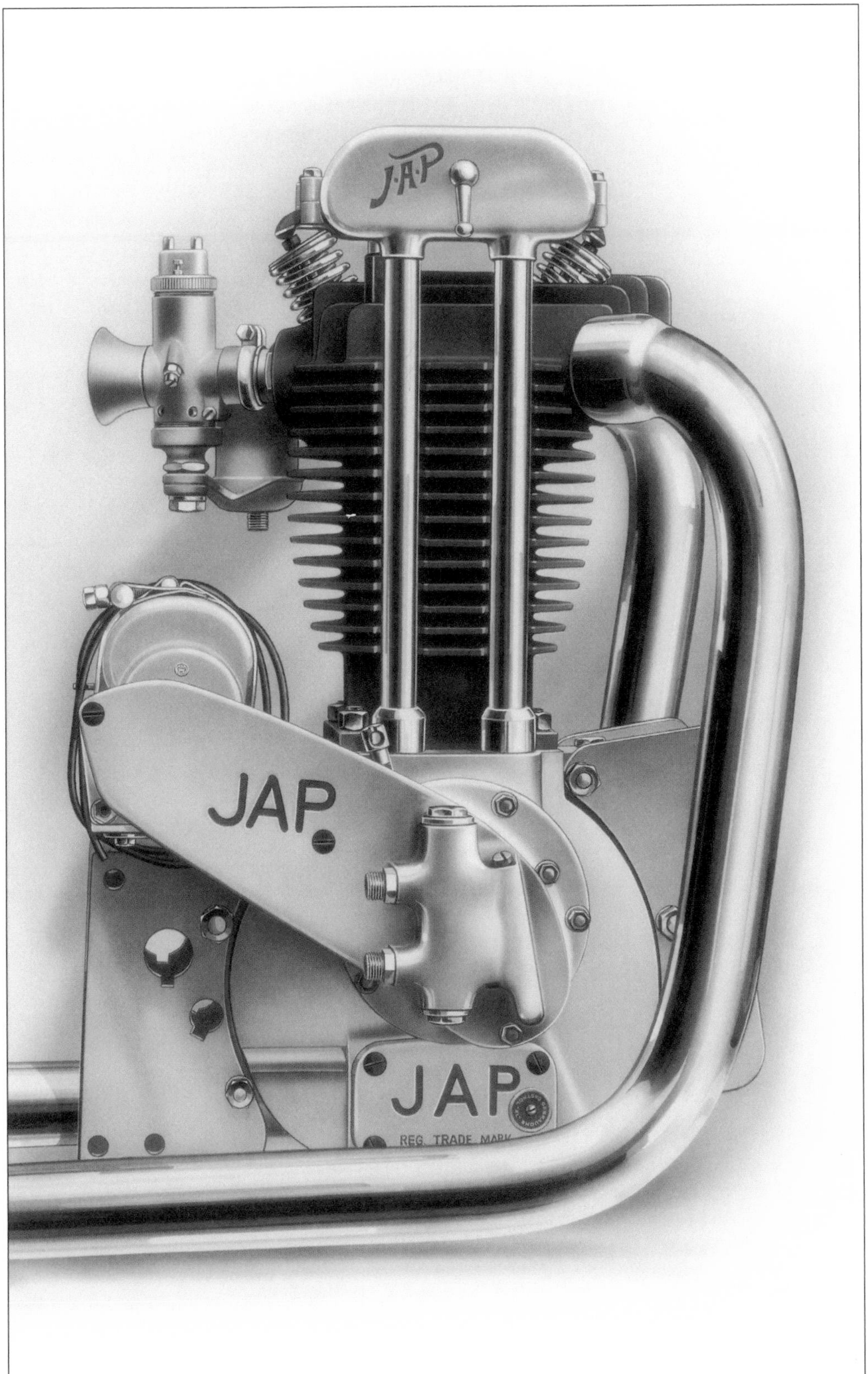
J·A·P
JAP
JAP
REG. TRADE MARK

Giovanni Boccaccio, ›Laurettas Florentiner Glass‹. Sketches of letters to be used in the manuscript HZ No. 45, dated Bordeaux, 4.4.44. The text mixes different uppercase letters, an idea that would be used again 50 years later in the digital ›Zapfino‹. The variation of the capital letters should express the caprices of Lauretta in a plastic way.

The manuscript fell into the hands of Russian soldiers at Schwarzenberg in Saxony. The title page was ripped out, as it contained an illustration of a graceful Florentine lady; but they had no use for the calligraphic pages. Through the help of friends in Schwarzenberg, and lengthy negotiation with the Russian commander, the fragment came back.

The Boccaccio manuscript was my first effort to bring variation to the capital letters' rigid system, which I would revisit many years later in the ›Zapfino‹ typeface.

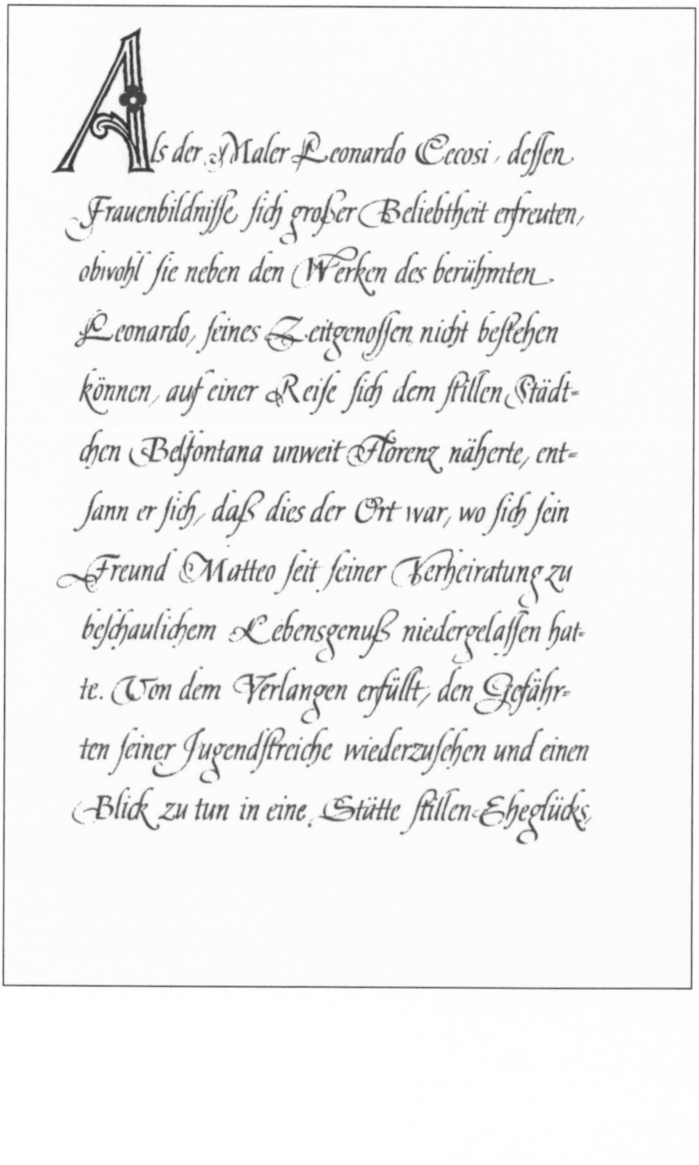
Als der Maler Leonardo Cecosi, deſſen
Frauenbildniſſe ſich großer Beliebtheit erfreuten,
obwohl ſie neben den Werken des berühmten
Leonardo, ſeines Zeitgenoſſen nicht beſtehen
können, auf einer Reiſe ſich dem ſtillen Städtchen Belfontana unweit Florenz näherte, ent-
ſann er ſich, daß dies der Ort war, wo ſich ſein
Freund Matteo ſeit ſeiner Verheiratung zu
beſchaulichem Lebensgenuß niedergelaſſen hat-
te. Von dem Verlangen erfüllt, den Gefähr-
ten ſeiner Jugendſtreiche wiederzuſehen und einen
Blick zu tun in eine Stätte ſtillen Eheglücks,

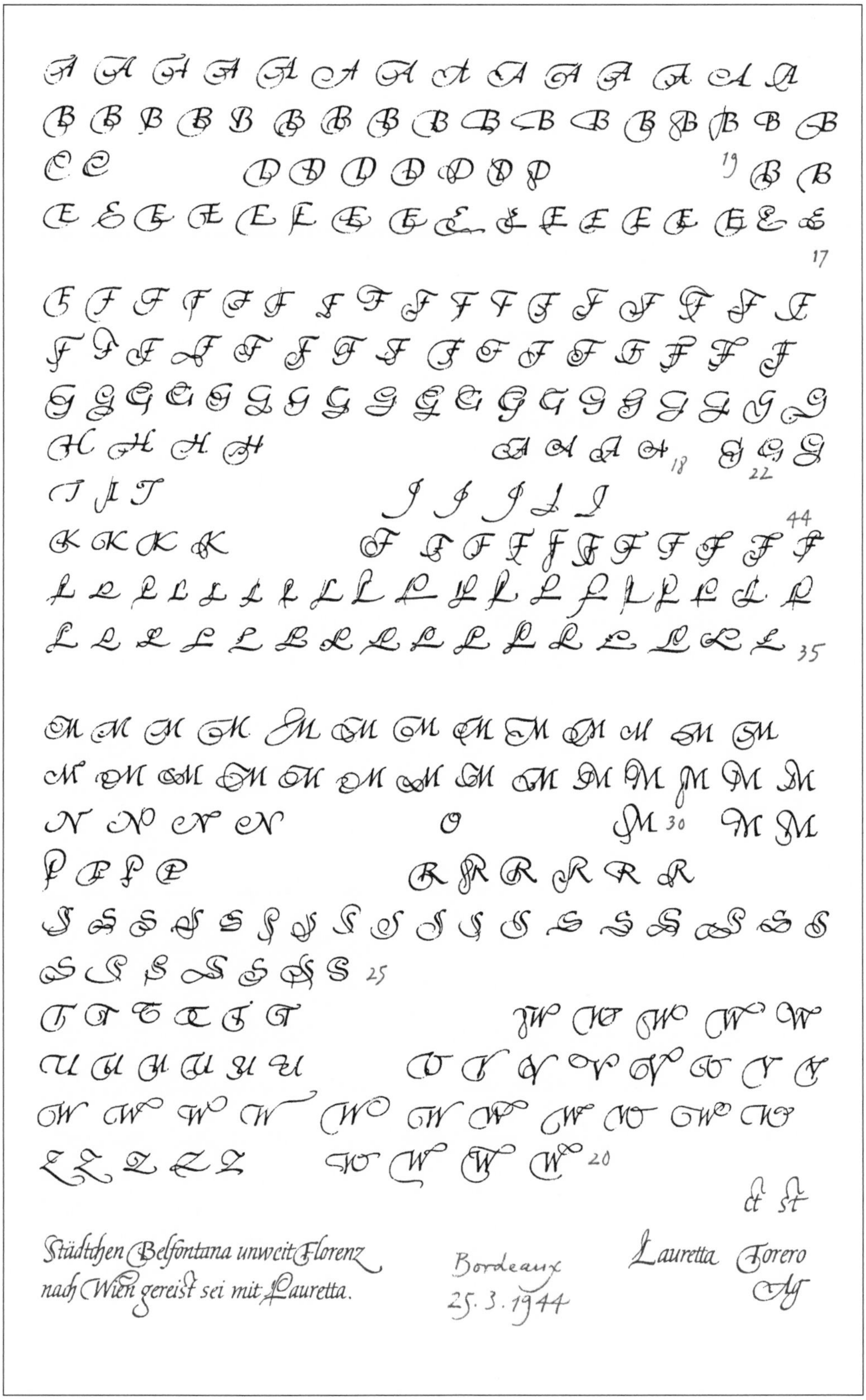
Städtchen Belfontana unweit Florenz
nach Wien gereist sei mit Lauretta.
Bordeaux
25.3.1944
Lauretta Torero

›Das Blumen-ABC von Hermann Zapf und August Rosenberger‹. The last page with the bryony flower.

The calligraphic text is a parable by Leonardo da Vinci on dissatisfaction. This was the only page that was finished for production; it was made as a calligraphy example for August Rosenberger. Other poems were planned to be typographically incised, together with the relevant flowers. The idea was to integrate text and image, flower poems bound together with drawings.

The illustration of the various plants and insects together compose the anagram H. Zapf: H = Hirschkäfer (stag beetle), Z = Zaunrübe (bryony), A = Akazie (acacia), P = Postillionfalter (postillion butterfly; lat. olias crocea), and F = Fliege (fly).

Translation: »The bryony unhappy with her fence was moving with her tendrils across the street to fasten herself at the fence opposite, whereupon she was torn by wanderers.«

Leonardo da Vinci:
Fluch der Unzufriedenheit

Die Zaunrübe, nicht zufrieden
mit ihrem Zaun,
begann

mit ihren
Ranken

über die Straße
zu wandern und sich
an den Zaun

Zaunrübe gegenüber
zu
hängen –

Worauf sie
von den Wanderern zerrissen wurde.)

(Aus dem Codice Atlantico)

Santa Croce, Florence. Pencil sketch of the façade of the Franciscan church, dated October 1950. Many examples of great art can be seen inside the building, including Giotto's frescos and the tomb of Michelangelo. On the bottom of the page are a few letters drawn from the beautiful gravestones of Florentine families. The raised letters in blue were added onto the page afterwards; these show already the typical forms of the later ›Optima Roman‹.

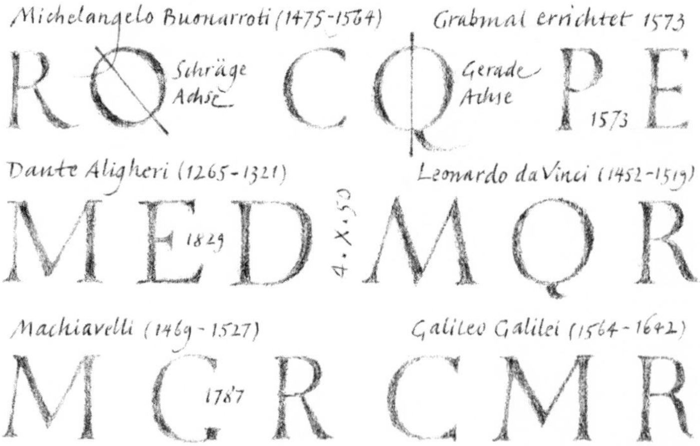

Some sketches from inscriptions in Santa Croce. Unfortunately, Italy's classic lettering tradition has degenerated since the middle of the 16th century.

Florenz
Santa Croce
Oktober 1950
ASTMGP
PRAMQ
ESR

›Optima Roman‹. Foundry proof of the pilot size, 36 point, printed on my 40th birthday at the D. Stempel AG type foundry in Frankfurt. Various corrections are marked by hand for the typeface's release.

The Optima made for hand composition had no italic, only an obliqued Roman slanted at 12 degrees. The digital version redesigned as ›Optima nova‹ in 2003 received a true italic, along with many additional characters that were unavailable in the metal typeface.

Drawing for an engraving in brass to be used on the binding of the book ›Das Reich der Wissenschaften‹ (The empire of science), written by Peter Halm and published by Hermann Emig in Amorbach, 1962.

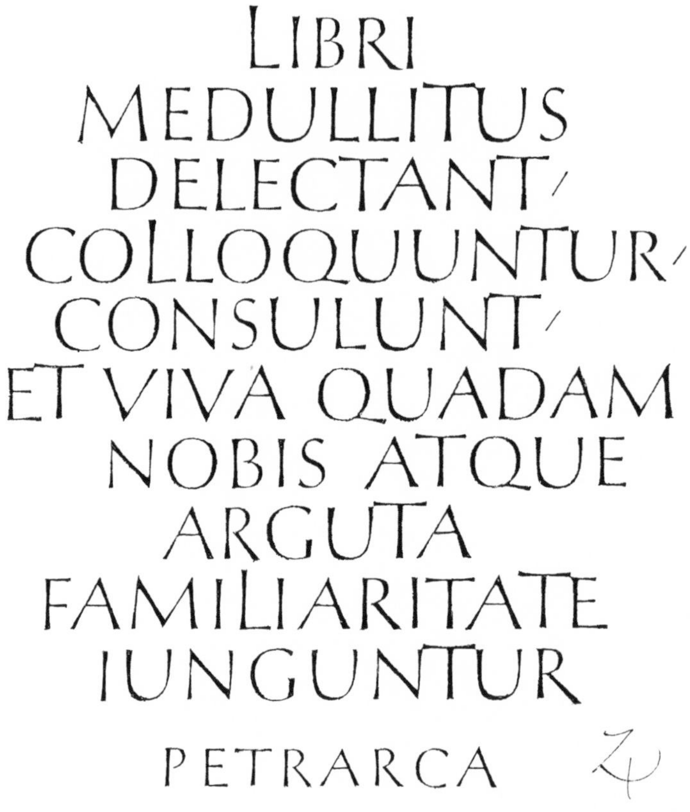
LIBRI
MEDULLITUS
DELECTANT,
COLLOQUUNTUR,
CONSULUNT,
ET VIVA QUADAM
NOBIS ATQUE
ARGUTA
FAMILIARITATE
IUNGUNTUR
PETRARCA

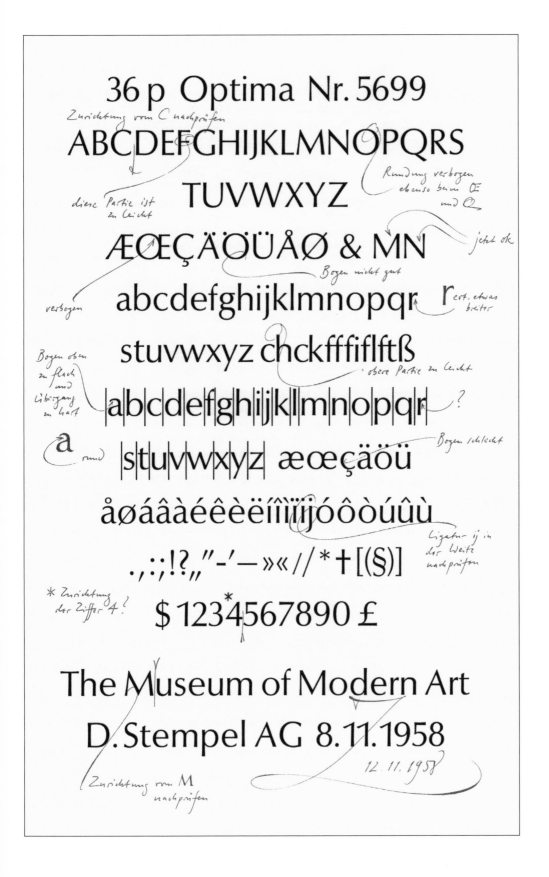

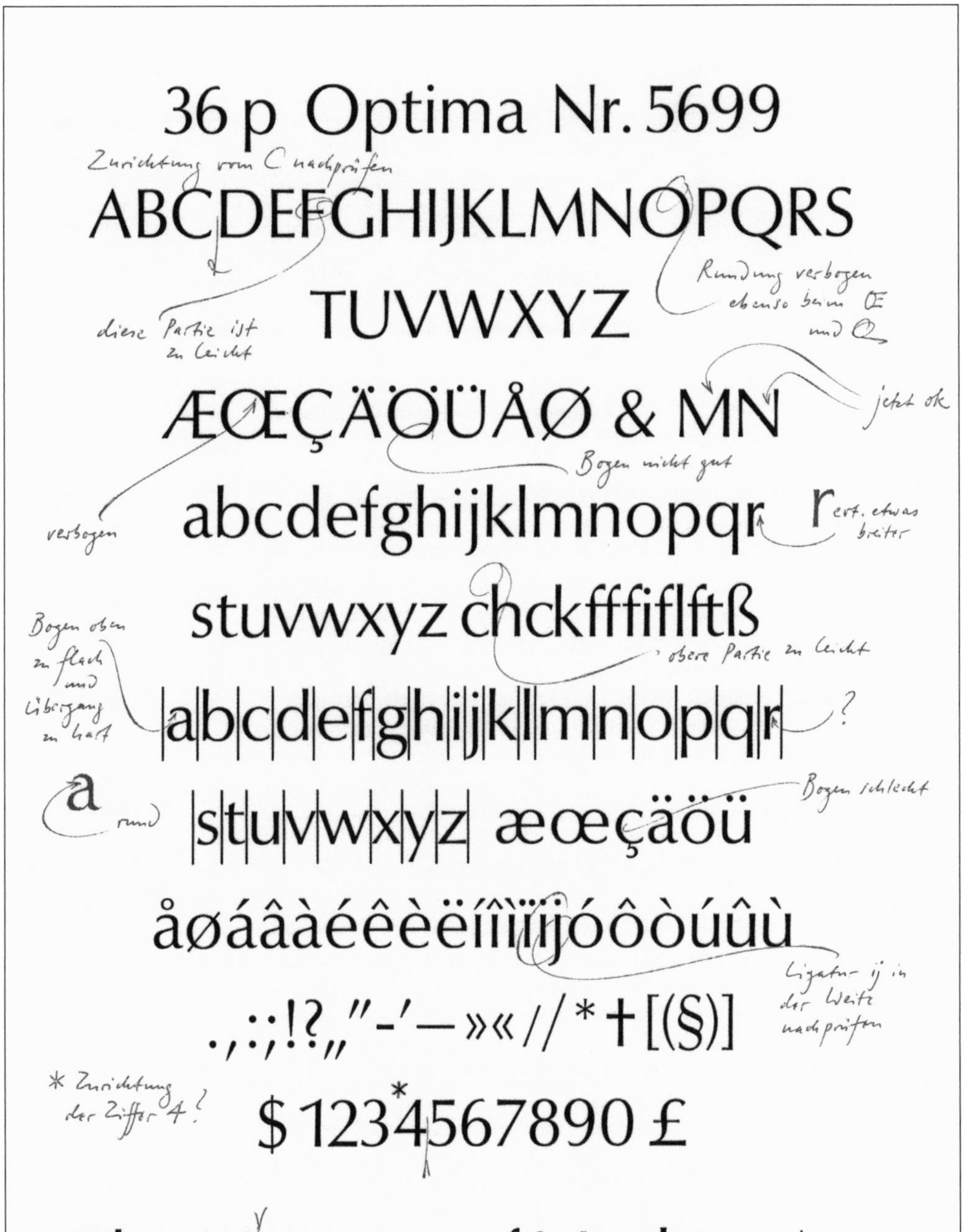
36 p Optima Nr. 5699
Zurichtung vom C nachprüfen
ABCDEFGHIJKLMNOPQRS
TUVWXYZ
diese Partie ist zu leicht
Rundung verbogen ebenso beim Œ und Q
ÆŒÇÄÖÜÅØ & MN
jetzt ok
Bogen nicht gut
abcdefghijklmnopqr
verbogen
r erst etwas breiter
stuvwxyz chckffffiflftß
obere Partie zu leicht
Bogen oben zu flach und Übergang zu hart
|a|b|c|d|e|f|g|h|i|j|k|l|m|n|o|p|q|r|
?
a rund
|s|t|u|v|w|x|y|z| æœçäöü
Bogen schlecht
åøáâàéêèëíîìïijóôòúûù
Ligatur ij in der Weite nachprüfen
.,:;!?„"-'—»«//*†[(§)]
* Zurichtung der Ziffer 4?
$1234567890£
The Museum of Modern Art
D. Stempel AG 8.11.1958
12.11.1958
Zurichtung vom M nachprüfen

›Virtuosa I & II‹. An ornamental script face developed for metal typesetting in 1948–1951. Virtuosa I was a version with decorated uppercase letters, while Virtuosa II had simplified capitals and was intended to be used in smaller sizes. Both alphabets were later accompanied by a bold design.

Due to technical considerations, Virtuosa's metal type letters could not be cast with connectors. But it was possible to fit several additional characters into the standard layout of the compositor's case.

In 1954, a Greek variant of Virtuosa was added. P.M. Steffanides from Nicosia, Cyrus, who was representing the Stempel foundry in Greece, even received permission for this typeface to be named ›Frederika‹, after the then-reigning Queen of Greece.

Frederika (Φρειδερίκη) Α Β Γ
Δ Ε Ζ Η Θ Ι Κ Λ Μ Ν Ξ
Ο Π Ρ Σ Τ Υ Φ Χ Ψ & Ω
αβγδεζηθικλμνξοπρσςτυφχψω @

Virtuosa I • A A B C D E F G H I I

J K L M M N O P Qu R S T T U

V V W X Y Z & Æ Œ Ç Ø St Vi AG

abcdefghijklmnopqurstuvwxyz gwyæckßtzffngnd

Virtuosa II • A B C D E F G H I J K

L M N O P Qu R S T U V W X Y Z

£ $ 1 2 3 4 5 6 7 8 9 0 V I X • Hermann Zapf

Kräftige Virtuosa • A B C D E F G

H I J K L M N O P Q R S T T

U V W X Y Z & Qu Æ Œ Ç Ø Th

1234567890 abcddefgghijklmnopqrstuvw

xyz & æchckßtznde • D. Stempel AG

›Al-ahram Arabic‹. Character overview of Al-ahram Arabic for the D. Stempel AG type foundry in Frankfurt; dated 1956, in Arabic. This typeface was designed especially for use in newspaper printing. To avoid technical problems, the typical kerning method for printed Arabic letters had to be avoided. The type was baptized ›Al-ahram‹ (the pyramid), after the biggest Arabic newspaper in Cairo.

The advantages of the new digital possibilities, especially in developing Arabic alphabets, can be seen in the redesigned Palatino Arabic, which is based on Al-ahram Arabic.

Arabic typefaces may now be created without technical restrictions and limitations; this is a great help for designers. The more calligraphic version of the Palatino Arabic was developed with Nadine Chahine from Beirut and finished in 2006.

For headlines and emphasis in advertising a special and attractive design was developed in 1957, but only for hand composition. ›Al-ahram Shadowed‹ was very successful for its three-dimensional appearance.

التاجر مجده فى كيسه
العالم مجده فى كراريسه

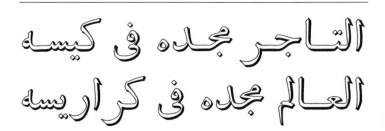

›The merchant takes pride in his purse, the scholar in his books.‹

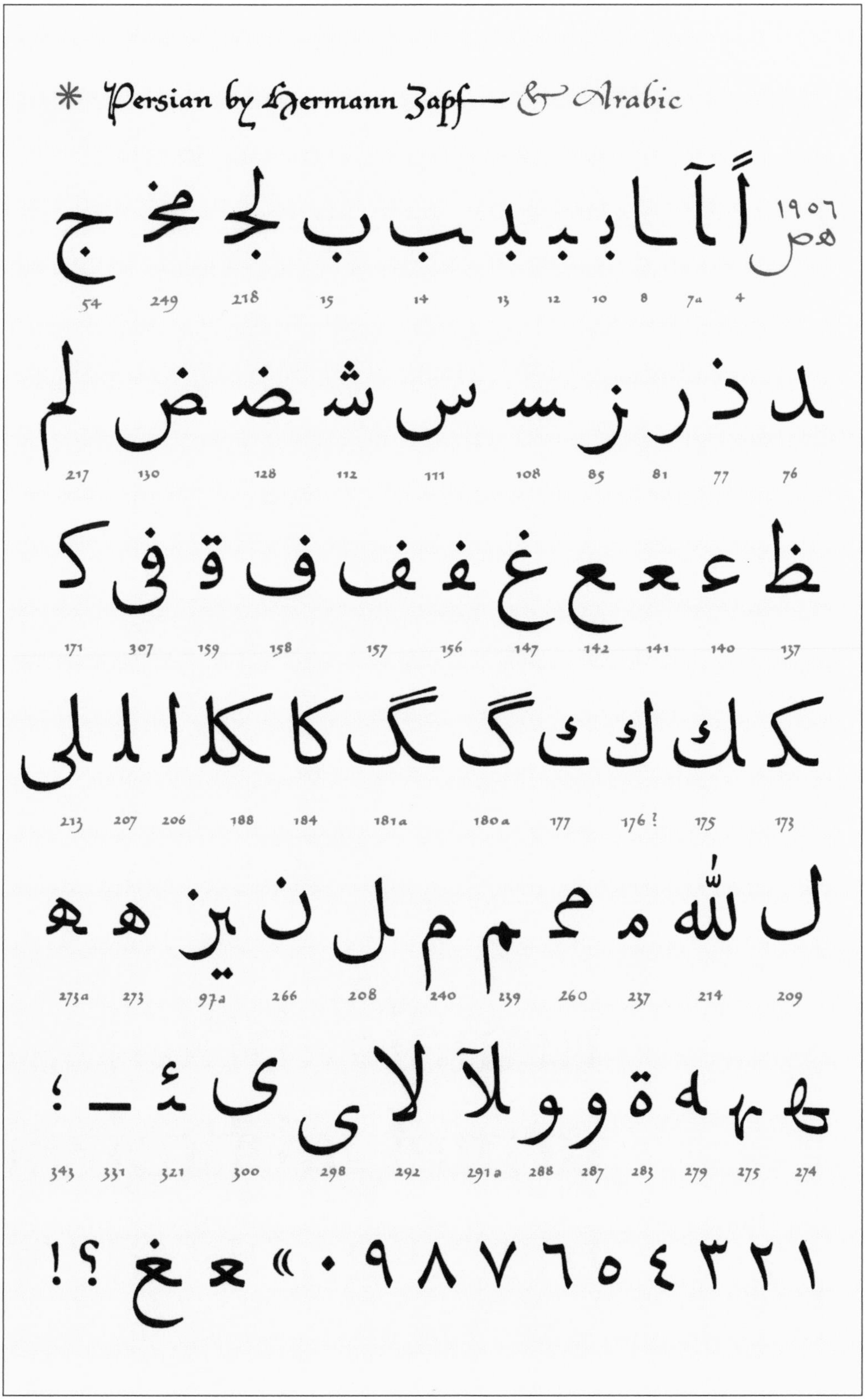
* Persian by Hermann Zapf — & Arabic
54 249 218 15 14 13 12 10 8 7a 4
217 130 128 112 111 108 85 81 77 76
171 307 159 158 157 156 147 142 141 140 137
213 207 206 188 184 181a 180a 177 176 ? 175 173
273a 273 97a 266 208 240 239 260 237 214 209
343 331 321 300 298 292 291a 288 287 283 279 275 274

›Linofilm Melior‹. A survey of the changes made to the foundry version of the ›Melior‹ typeface in 1966. These allowed it to be used with the Linofilm photosetting system ›Linotron 505‹. Unfortunately, it was not possible to extend the redesign to include elongating the short descenders or making the top right curve of the f any wider. At the bottom of the image is a reference made many years later to the ›super ellipse‹, mathematically developed by Piet Hein in Denmark in 1959.

The creation of Melior included intensive studies of legibility and printing on newspaper presses with liquid ink. I began these in 1948. To ensure the quick reading of information in a newspaper, readability is paramount. The rounded letters were designed within the middle form of a circle and square, but without any mathematical considerations of the later named ›super ellipse‹.

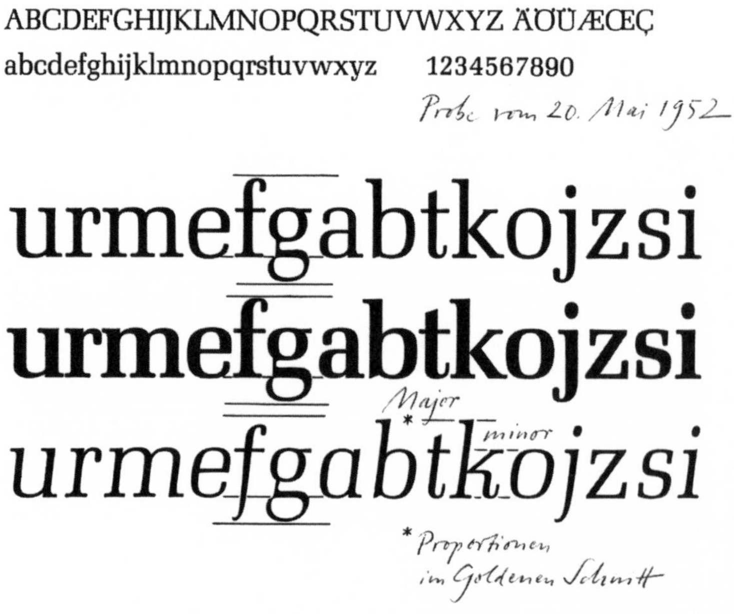

LINOFILM – MELIOR *

Copyright by Hermann Zapf 1966

serifs sharper for photocomposition

A B C D E F G H I J K L M N

cross stroke deeper — new design — hairlines not so heavy in Linofilm Melior

serifs more crisp, not so soft

O P Q R S T U V W X Y Z

new spine — redesigned form — old form for comparison

Ä Ö Ü É Ê È Ë Æ Œ Ç Ø Å

old form for comparison — larger (see Italic)

new design — bracketed serifs, not too round

a b c d e f g h i j k l m n o p q

old form for comparison — loop wider — new design — old forms for comparison

serifs a little longer

r s t u v w x y z ß ch ck ä ö ü

new designs — hairlines thinner — new design — separate see ligatures in Melior Italic

new head

ff fi fl ft á â à é ê è ë í î ì ï ó ô ò

old form for comparison

old form for comparison — shorter — shorter

ú û ù æ œ ç ø å ij 1 2 3 4 5 6 7

new design — new design

8 9 0 £ $ & . , - : ; ! ? ' ( ) „ " » « /

shorter

– [ ] § †

To understand the general principle of MELIOR please study the story about Piet Hein's SUPERELLIPSE, a mathematical construction of 1959, in » Scientific American «, September 1965, pp. 222–236.

(Melior was designed 1948/49)

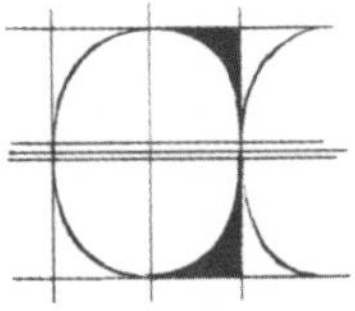

* = junction of the curves was too heavy

(6pt = 20 12pt = 40)

Z 24·2·1966

* also for LINOTRON 505

›Manuale Typographicum‹ 1968. Page composed in ›Sistina Titling‹, with a text in which the words were arranged alphabetically. (Taken from the writing manual by Johanes Muscat, published in Nuremberg around 1650. The quotation, from Martin Luther, is from »Tischreden oder Colloquia«, vol. 4, Berlin, 1848, p. 715).

›Sistina‹ was developed in 1950, after studies of inscriptions in Rome, as an all caps alphabet for the ›Palatino‹ project. Cut by the punchcutter August Rosenberger for the D. Stempel AG typefoundry in Frankfurt. The largest size ever cast was 84 point, or 22 mm.

In addition to ›Sistina‹, the much lighter ›Michelangelo‹ was cut. This was also a titling face, and designed in 1950. Redesigns of Michelangelo and Sistina were made in 2005 in connection with the ›Palatino nova‹ type family. A Greek alphabet named ›Phidias‹ based on Michelangelo was first released by D. Stempel AG in 1952.

ABCDEFGHI
JKLMNOPQRST
UVWXYZ
& KRQUWYZ ST TH
1234567890
*
ΑΒΓΔΕΖΗΘΙ
ΚΛΜΝΞΟΠΡΣΤΥ
ΦΧΨΩ

ΑΡΧΗ ΜΕΓΙΣΤΗ ΤΟΥ
ΒΙΟΥ ΤΑ ΓΡΑΜΜΑΤΑ

JOHANN
MUSCAT ✠ A A BONO B CHRISTO C

DEI D ELECTO E FILIO/ F GENERIS

G HUMANI H IMMANUELE/ I LIBERA-

TORE/ L MEDIATORE M NOSTRO N

O OMNIA P PENITUS QV QUIA

R REPARATA S SUNT ✠ T TU U

UTERE X XRISTO KYRIO CUM
ZELO Z

Die Druckerey ist summum et postremum donum, durch welches GOTT die sache des Evangelii forttreibet. Es ist die letzte Flamme vor dem Auslöschen der welt. Sie ist, GOTT lob am Ende.

✠ MARTIN
LUTHER

›Zapf Renaissance Italic‹. The Italic version of ›Renaissance Roman‹, designed for Scangraphic D. Böger GmbH in Hamburg. The type family was developed especially for the ›Scantext 1000‹ CRT typesetting machine. Already in 1984, this system allowed for the addition of extra characters and alternates, as well as for kerning and the overlapping of letters.

When I began working on this alphabet, I wanted to study handwritten humanist manuscripts in the Laurenziana in Florence. Of course, I did not have credentials from any famous art institution to present upon my arrival there. After a fruitless conversation with the librarian, I wrote »LM« – for Lorenzo di Medici – in large letters on the ticket. Then in my bad Italian, I introduced myself: »I am a calligrapher from Germany«. After very carefully examining the two letters I had drawn, a smile came over his face. At once, he opened up all of the treasures of the Medici for me. Only two letters were enough. He kept my ticket.

Zapf Renaissance Buch

ABCDEFGHIJKLMNOPQ
RSTUVWXYZ
abcdefghijklmnopqrstuvwxyz

ABCDEFGHIJKLMNOPQ
RSTUVWXYZ
abcdefghijklmnopqrstuvwxyz

Zapf Renaissance Bold

Zapf Renaissance Italic ❧ TABVLA ABCDARIÆ

a a b c d d e e e f f f g g g g h i j k k

¶ A B C D E F G H I J K L M N O

l m m n n o p p p q r r r s s s t t t u

P Q R S T U V W X Y Z ❧ Æ Œ

u v v v w w w x x y y y z z z & fi ff

¶ A B C D E F G H I J K L M

fl ß ff ffi ffl ll qu th sp st & b d h k l ❧

N O P Q R S T U V W X Y Z

❧ 1234567890 ❧ $12,345,678.90¢

❧

Typographic Computer Programs. Page 121 is a trial page of the planned ›Manuale Photo-Typographicum‹. A 1967 proposal shows a design grid with an illustration inside its building-block system. First published in ›Book design in the past and future‹, by Hermann Zapf. From ›Homage to the book‹, West Virginia Pulp and Paper Company, New York 1968. Photo: Herb Weitman, ›Lithopinion‹, New York.

An illustration of a poster for the Rochester Institute of Technology, School of Printing Management and Sciences, created for American universities and corporations. The image is shown at a very reduced size.

Rochester Institute of Technology: HERMANN ZAPF *is teaching*
TYPOGRAPHIC COMPUTER PROGRAMS
June 21 - July 2, 1982

»The development of special grid and modular programs for various typographic applications, tailored for economic book production and magazine design. An advanced course of study designed to raise standards and explore the new structures of formatting for computerized and program oriented photo-composition«.

C B A

BOOK DESIGN IN THE FUTURE

1

The growth in production will bring great changes in today's working rules. Is it really unrealistic to believe that production of standard books, and especially of pocket books, will be solved by computers?

1

This enormous variety of possibilities leads us to new thoughts, new considerations:

Computerized composition will also change some aspects of the printing industry. Page and volume calculation can be done by the computer in extremely short periods of time, thus effecting economics in production by changing the measure of type and the leading. This, of course, requires certain suppositions which we will have to accept in the future.

The time is not far when the manuscript – hand- or typewritten – will be put into a reading machine which, via a computer, produces the information necessary for book production on paper- or magnetic tape. The computer will also be programmed to correct automatically typographic and grammatical errors, check the logic of thoughts, prepare an index of names and conceptions, compare dates and even translate a complete work into any foreign language.

2

All the same, we should face the new trend realistically: computers have not done away with any methods as yet, they have only changed them. Of necessity, computer-typography is bound to be more exact than the orthodox work of a compositor. Without fail, the automated machine works to the programmed instructions fed into it, putting in running heads, chapter headings and folios, captions and subtitles, picking out references and footnotes, eliminating widows and hyphenations breaking over a page, performing other typographical chores.

3

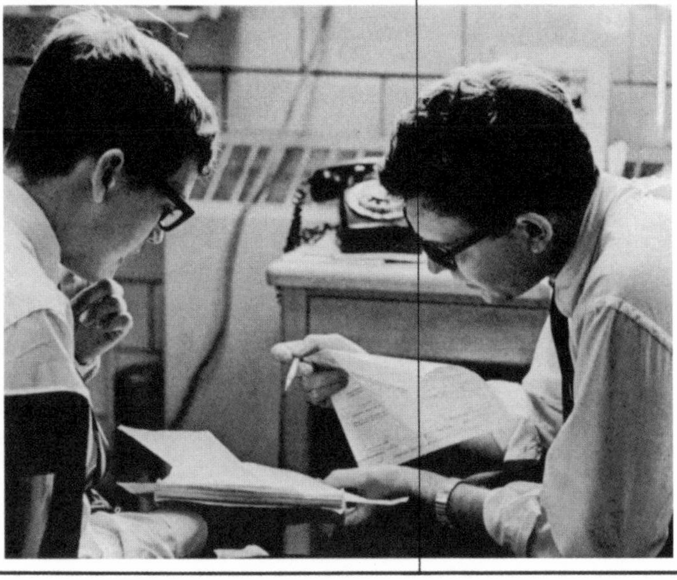

What we need are clear concepts in typography – book designs aimed at legibility and clarity, free of unnecessary extras. The disappearance of superfluous ornaments and frills in favor of simplicity need not in any way produce a sterile typographic outlook.

5

Asymmetrischer Grid Modul basierend auf den Fibonacci Zahlen
1 - 1 - 2 - 3 - 5 (senkrecht) und 3 - 5 - 8 (waagerecht).

1967

›*hz*-Program‹. Page from the first announcement of the *hz*-Program in 1990. As a comparison, the same text is shown in two versions. One is created via traditional typesetting, and another with the improved level of quality made possible by the *hz*-Program. After 38 lines, a whole line was saved.

Some features of the *hz*-Program have been included in Adobe ›InDesign®‹, but without any reference to it.

The disadvantage of the *hz*-Program in 1990 was an approximately seven percent reduction in composition speed. In the eyes of professionals, this was much too slow. Speed played such an important role in composition. The other problem at the time was that it required too much memory.

A diagram of the type area of Gutenberg's 42-line Bible. (After Raúl M. Rosarivo's ›Divina Proportio Typografica‹. A publication of the golden typographic module 1:1.5 in the proportion 2:3, the module of Johannes Gutenberg and his contemporaries).
Published by Richard Scherpe Verlag, Krefeld, 1961.

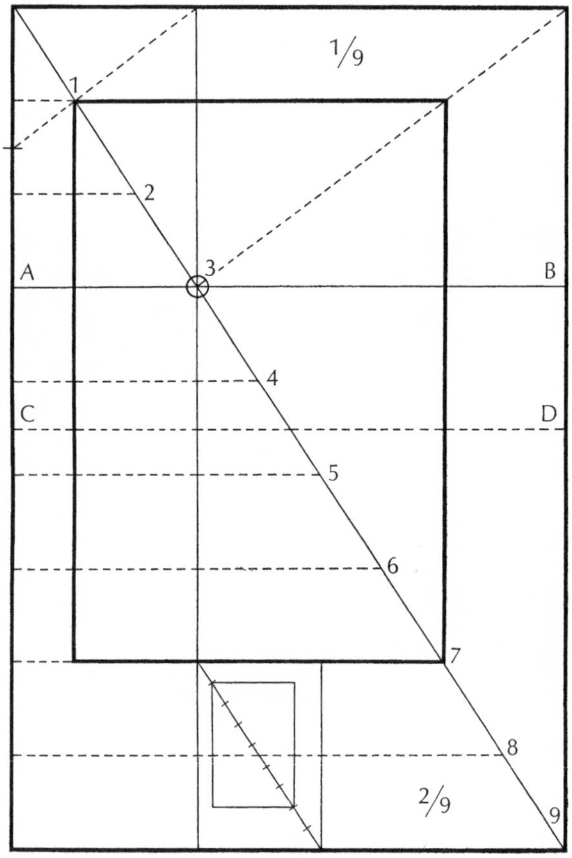

The Secret of Gutenberg

What makes the Gutenberg Bible the unattainable masterpiece of the art of printing? The printing on a hand-press? Not really, because of today's standards, the inking was not of extraordinary quality. We could order hand-made rag paper also in our day. Maybe the secret of his beautiful pages is in the proportions of the columns on the paper. But this we are also able to copy. Therefore only the composition is to be considered.

How could Gutenberg get those even grey areas of his columns without disturbing or unsightly holes between words? His secret: the master achieved this perfection by using several characters of different width combined with many ligatures and abbreviations in his type case. He finally created 290 characters for the composition of the 42-line Bible. An enormous time consuming job to realize his idea of good typographic lines: the justified lines of even length, compared to the flush-left lines of the works of the famous mediaeval scribes.

But with Johannes Gutenberg's unusual ligatures and abbreviations, today we can't use this principle for contemporary composition. Now we can get help through the versatility of modern electronic software and formats to receive a perfect type area in our production, to get closer to Gutenberg's standards of quality: The *hz*-Program of URW.

What makes the Gutenberg Bible the unattainable masterpiece of the art of printing? The printing on a hand-press? Not really, because of today's standards, the inking was not of extraordinary quality. We could order hand-made rag paper also in our day. Maybe the secret of his beautiful pages is in the proportions of the columns on the paper. But this we are also able to copy. Therefore only the composition is to be considered.

How could Gutenberg get those even grey areas of his columns without disturbing or unsightly holes between words? His secret: the master achieved this perfection by using several characters of different width combined with many ligatures and abbreviations in his type case. He finally created 290 characters for the composition of the 42-line Bible. An enormous time consuming job to realize his idea of good typographic lines: the justified lines of even length, compared to the flush-left lines of the works of the famous mediaeval scribes.

But with Johannes Gutenberg's unusual ligatures and abbreviations, today we can't use this principle for contemporary composition. Now we can get help through the versatility of modern electronic software and formats to receive a perfect type area in our production, to get closer to Gutenberg's standards of quality: The *hz*-Program of URW.

There are many applications for normal line length in book work. But considerable improvements are also possible in narrower columns for magazine designs.

Left column: Regular typesetting. Right column: Composition using the URW hz-Program.

The lowercase characters used for the 42-line Bible by Johannes Gutenberg, printed in Mainz about 1455.

Gottfried Wilhelm Leibniz. Philosopher, mathematician, and scholar. He developed the theory of infinitesimal calculus, which he presented in 1675 to the Royal Society in London.

In 1676, he was named librarian for the Duke Johann Friedrich of Brunswick-Lüneburg's collection in Hanover. After 1691, he became the court librarian for Duke August in Wolfenbüttel.

At the age of 29, Leibniz invented the binary system with the numbers 0 and 1, the basis of today's computer technology. He was corresponding with over 1,000 of the scholars of his time, from 15 different countries. More than 15,000 letters are stored in the Leibniz archive in Hanover.

My admiration for Gottfried Wilhelm Leibniz is shown in a special print from 2001, in a German and English edition. The English translation is dedicated to Donald E. Knuth, professor of Computer Programming, Stanford University.

Reproduction of the Leibniz calculating machine, seen from the bottom. This was the beginning of everything, nearly 300 years before the first programmable computer was constructed: the ›Z3‹ from Konrad Zuse in Berlin, 1941.

* Gottfried Wilhelm Leibniz (1646–1716) laid the foundations for electronics and today's computer technology, as well for cybernetics, with the invention of a binary system of notation.

Hommage à Leibniz

In 1675 Leibniz presented an explanation of infinitesimal calculus using an ink blot: The task was to measure the total area converted by the blot. Leibniz hit upon the idea of dividing the surface into diminutive units. These square units could then be calculated. But there were some elements whose surfaces were only partially covered by the contours of the blot. These could not be determined exactly. Using his infinitesimal calculus Leibniz progressively reduced the surfaces of these elements until there were almost no elements left with only partially covered surfaces. Mathematical calculation thus became possible.

Leibniz believed that the ›Characters of Fu-Hsi‹ contained the remnants of a binary arithmetic system which had been discovered thousands of years ago and then forgotten. He traced his own notation system, which is the basis of today's cybernetics, back to prehistoric China.

The 8 trigrams from the I-Ching

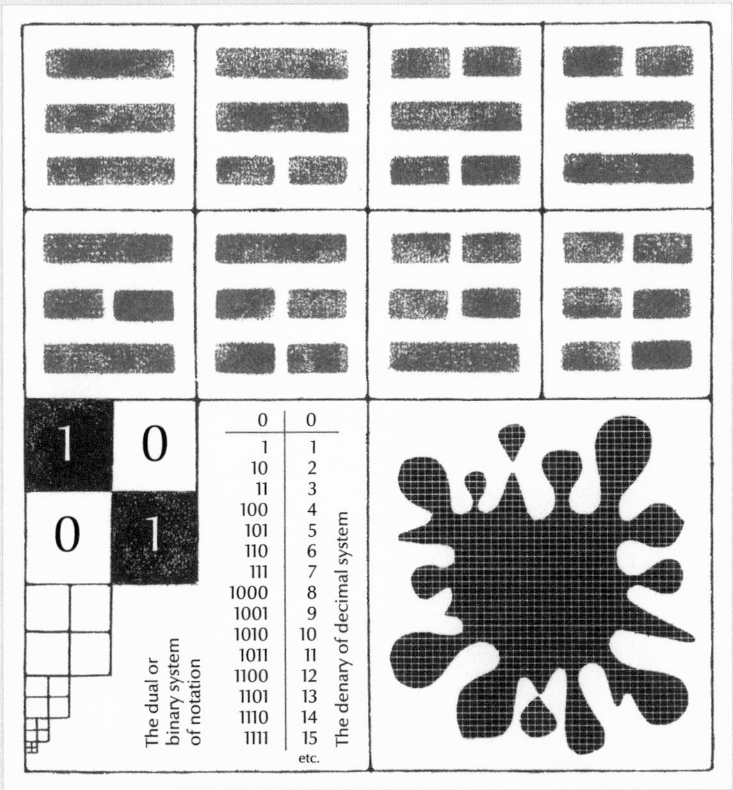

1
0
0
1
The dual or binary system of notation
0 | 0
1 | 1
10 | 2
11 | 3
100 | 4
101 | 5
110 | 6
111 | 7
1000 | 8
1001 | 9
1010 | 10
1011 | 11
1100 | 12
1101 | 13
1110 | 14
1111 | 15
etc.
The denary of decimal system

In principle the ink blot which Leibniz divided up into diminutive elements already resembles the digital raster – called a bitmap – which is used to regulate the pixels for letters in modern typesetting machines and laser printers.

Leibniz saw the binary System as a system underlying Creation. He imagined that the number one represented God and that zero stood for the void, and that the highest of all beings drew all other beings out of the void, just as one and zero express all numbers in this system. (Pierre Laplace)

Gottfried Wilhelm Leibniz to Duke Rudolf August of Brunswick-Lüneburg-Wolfenbüttel on 2nd January 1697: »... one of the main articles of the Christian faith ... is the creation of all things out of nothing by the omnipotence of God. Now one can very well say that nothing in the world represents this better, indeed virtually demonstrates it, than the origin of numbers, as it is presented here in their expression simply and solely by one and zero or nothing, and it would surely be hard to find a better model of this secret in nature or philosophy ...«

Wolfenbüttel, 26th June 1708, in a letter to Jacques Lelong: »... In time this new calculus system will be widely used because everything in it follows on from one simple rule.«

›Zapfino Hyper-flourishes‹. Drawings for the small caps in ›Zapfino‹ and proposals for extra-long swashes. This was my attempt in 1998 to break through the still extent typographic rules, which had dated back to the days of metal type and time immemorial, and which were responsible for the fixing of the design of a letter into a rectangular type body.

Today's digital technology makes such unrestricted solutions possible. Letters may run over two or three lines; but of course, some typographic ability is still needed to avoid arrangements that run wild. One example with a large descender on the letter y is shown on page 77. Who would have ever thought that such artwork could be made on a computer?

A small selection of 100 ornament designs for ›Zapfino Extra‹.

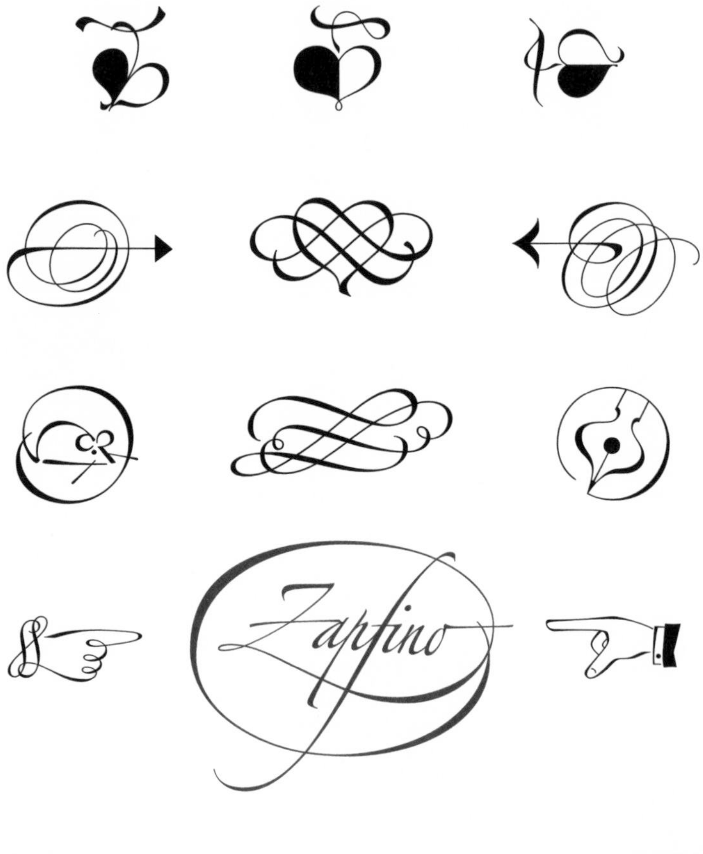

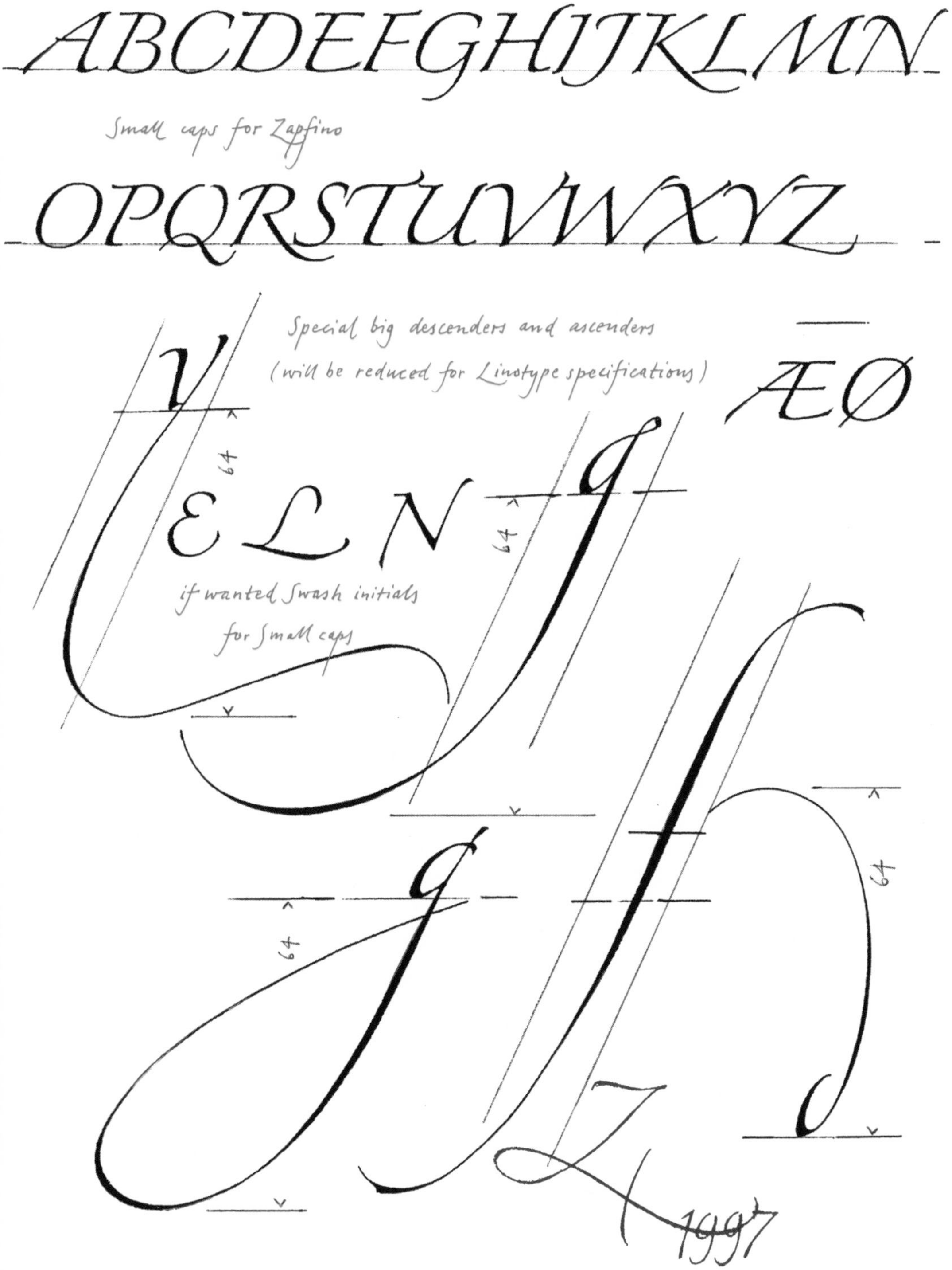
ABCDEFGHIJKLMN
Small caps for Zapfino
OPQRSTUVWXYZ
Special big descenders and ascenders
(will be reduced for Linotype specifications)
ÆØ
ELN
if wanted Swash initials
for Small caps
64
1997

Dynamic letters. The unlimited freedom of calligraphy can be seen on this sheet. Interlocking letters, individually and spontaneously arranged, fully following the imagination of the scribe, have been executed with different writing tools. The letters in sepia are written with a quill. The red and blue letters were made with colored pencils. The lines of text are written with a Parker fountain pen in black ink.

Miguel de Cervantes Saavedra: the alphabet of the attributes of a lover, taken from ›Don Quixote‹.

Many more feelings and emotions can be expressed in calligraphy than can ever be shown with typefaces. The example below was made with a pointed brush and without any guidelines. It is a text by Carl Michael Bellmann, written on a paper napkin at the ›Gyldene Freden‹ restaurant in Stockholm, 1968.

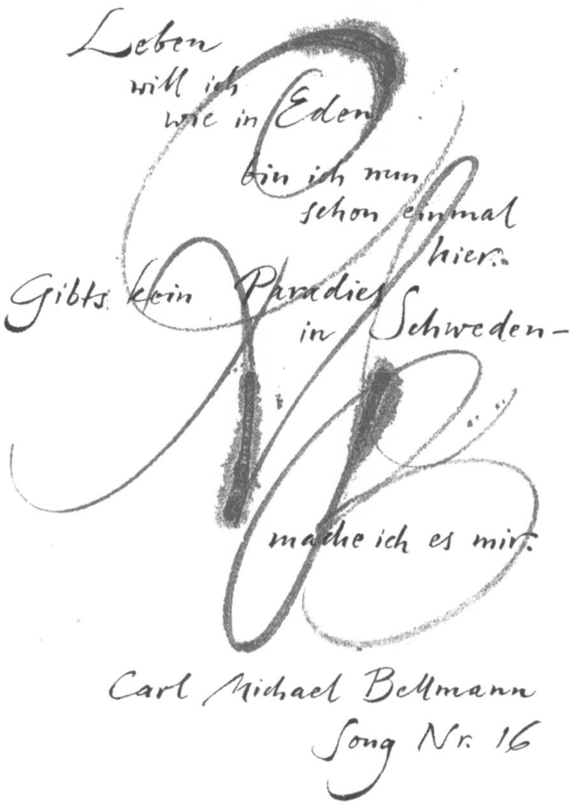
Leben
will ich
wie in Eden
bin ich nun
schon einmal
hier.
Gibts kein Paradies
in Schweden –
mache ich es mir.
Carl Michael Bellmann
Song Nr. 16

Required in every good lover the whole alphabet ...
Agreeable · Bountiful · Constant · Dutiful · Easy ·
Faithful · Gallant · Honourable · Ingenious · Kind ·
Loyal · Mild · Noble · Officious · Prudent ·
Quit · Rich · Secret · True · Valiant · Wise
Young and Zealous
Miguel de Cervantes ›Don Quixote‹

›Optima nova Titling‹. An overview of all 84 characters from a supplement to the Optima nova family, designed in 2003. The details of the individual letters are particularly noticeable in larger point sizes. Unusual logos, signets, and initials are welcome applications for Optima nova Titling.

Some examples of ›Zapf Essentials‹, which was developed at the same time as ›Optima nova‹, are shown combined with the type below.

ZAPF ESSENTIALS™ are digital dingbats and ornaments designed for every day use and as the name says, you just have to have them! There are endless possibilities for their use, as the font contains 372 designs with a variety of current, updated symbols for telephones, cell phones, telefax and e-mail.
Zapf Essentials feature a number of special characteristics. Besides masculine hands there are also gentler ladies' hands. (In the old days only men's hands were available, mostly solid.) And there are quick arrows with fading tails to show speed.
Zapf Essentials consist of a large variety of applications. In alphabetical order: Aldus leaves / adornments / arrows / boxes / bullets / cutters / currency signs € / decorations / extras / emphasizers / eye-catchers / fleurons / fingers / fillers / flourishes / geometrical elements / glyphs / hands (feminine and masculine) / indexes / indicators / markers / ornaments / pointers / scissors / signals / signs / separators / shouters / stars / symbols / three dimensionals etc.
Zapf Essentials should be used sparingly to highlight important parts of a text. The shown examples are for display only and should not be taken as models, but there are no limits to your imagination!
Have fun with Zapf Essentials!

Optima nova Titling with all special characters

The complete font includes accented letters, punctuations, etc.

›Palatino nova‹. Page from the 2005 Linotype GmbH type specimen showing all characters from the font, including the extras and those for mathematics. The typeface is equipped with four figure styles. First, there are standard numbers for tables, as well as proportional-width figures. Also, the oldstyle figures have two versions as well. These should always be used within text matter. Bullets, hyphens, and dashes are available in two different heights: one for strings of capitals and another for text.

A selection of glyphs from ›Palatino nova Italic‹, whose character set was significantly redesigned and enlarged when compared with the old metal version from 1953.

ABCDEFGHIJKLMN

OPQRSTUVWXYZ & Æ Œ

@abcdefghijklmnop

qrstuvwxyz ct et sp st & æ œ

fi fl ij ft fj ff fh ffi ffl fft ß

0123456789 0123456789

€ ₵ $ ¢ £ ¥

ABCDEFGHIJKLMN

OPQRSTUVWXYZ & 1234567890

1st 2nd 3rd 4th 1ST 2ND 3RD 4TH

Palatino nova

¶ ABCDEFGHIJKLMNOPQRST
UVWXYZ & ÆŒ *

@abcdefghijklmnopqrstuvwxyz

æ œ ß fi fl ij ft fj ff fh ffi ffl fft & ct ct sp st *

Tabular lining figures 0123456789° 0123456789 Proportional lining figures

Tabular Oldstyle figures 0123456789…0123456789 Proportional Oldstyle figures

€ ₵ $ ¢ £ ¥ ¤ . , : ; ” „ “ ’ » « › ‹ ? ! ¿ ¡ # † ‡ § ' "

Small Caps ABCDEFGHIJKLMNOPQRSTUVWXYZ
1234567890 & € $ ₵ £ ƒ ¥ * † ‡ § ‖ ¶ English footnotes

H abcdegilmnorst H 1234567890/1234567890

1st 2nd 3rd 4th th 1ST 2ND 3RD 4TH TH © ® TM

H • H · H - H – H — H h - h – h — h † h ‡ h

[({ % ‰ ¼ ½ ¾ })] / | \ ¦ ‖ ∂ µ π Δ Ω

∑ √ + − ± · × ÷ ¬ = ≠ ≈ ~ < > ≤ ≥ ∞ ∫ ∏

List of the redesign 2002–2005. In total 671 Glyphs

›Palatino Sans Italic‹. The Sans alphabet has two different designs, named ›Palatino Sans‹ and ›Palatino Sans Informal‹. The regular Sans alphabet becomes more lively, personal, and expressive in the Sans Informal version. The differences are especially noticeable in the letters a, f, g, and p. Between samples of Palatino Sans Italic and Palatino Sans Informal Italic, a showing of Palatino Sans Ultra Light Italic has been printed.

This new addition to the Palatino type family was first shown in a Linotype type specimen in 2006. The specimen includes a reprint of an interesting essay by Walter Tracy, London, ›The origin of the term Sans‹, as well as a historical survey of 65 years of computer development, from Konrad Zuse's invention of the ›Z3‹ in Berlin up to Apple's ›iPod‹ in 2006. Also included is a list of most of my known typefaces, from ›Gilgengart Fraktur‹, 1938, to ›Zapfino Ink‹, designed in 2006.

The refinement of the drawings for the Palatino Sans alphabets can be seen best in larger sizes, of course. But in smaller sizes, the impression of the Sans is more human in comparison with ordinary sans serif types, which are usually made up of completely straight lines drawn with a ruling pen and a ruler, intentionally turning away from the customary principle of construction.

HE NE NN OO ST ND AT ET

For ›Palatino Sans Ultra Light‹, several unusual capital letter ligatures were added, as well as a series of funny arrows for use in ads, all kinds of print ephemera, signals, pointers, and marks. These arrows can be used not only with the Palatino Sans designs, but also with other alphabets. However, they should be used sparingly. This same bit of advice applies to the capital ligatures as well.

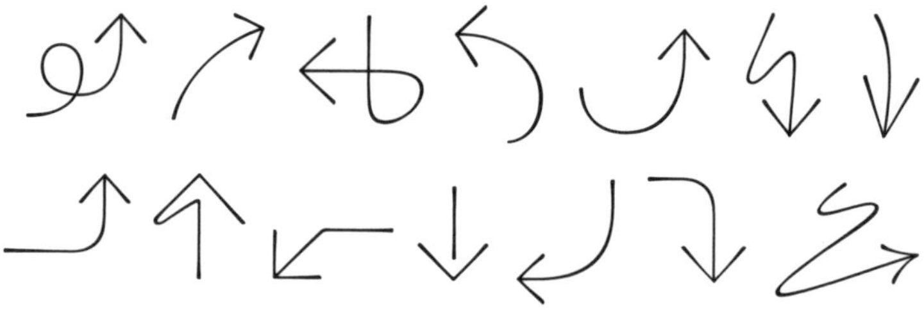

Palatino Sans Italic

ABCDEFGHIJKLMNOPQRST
UVWXYZ & ÆŒ
abcdefghijklmnopqrstuvwxyz
æ œ fi fl ij ft ff ct et sp st tt tz th

ABCDEFGHIJKLMNOPQRST
UVWXYZ & ÆŒ
abcdefghijklmnopqrstuvwxyz
æ œ fi fl ij ft ff ct et sp st tt tz th

ABCDEFGHIJKLMNOPQRST
UVWXYZ & ÆŒ
abcdefghijklmnopqrstuvwxyz
æ œ fi fl ij ft ff ct et sp st tt tz th

Palatino Sans Informal Italic

›Palatino Sans Ultra Light‹. The manifold range of assignments undertaken in advertising often call for unusual contrast and effects. Palatino Sans Ultra Light was originally developed as a design concept in 1973, but at that time, there was no interest or demand for such an ultra light expression within the sans serif genre. Perhaps in the 1970s, sans serifs were mostly used for information and not as much for effective contrast or even the elegance of their letters.

The quotation by Paul Standard (1896–1992) is composed of asymmetrical lines set in Palatino Sans Ultra Light, together with Palatino nova Light for the German translation. (Bibliography: ›Manuale Typographicum 1954‹, p. 63).

Before my first trip to America in 1951, I was already corresponding with Paul Standard. In connection with my joint exhibition with Fritz Kredel, I finally met both personally for the first time in New York. Over the following years, we would exchange many letters. The Melbert B. Cary, Jr. Graphic Arts Collection at RIT published a booklet with my calligraphic letter headings under the title ›Calligraphic Salutations‹, with a preface by David Pankow (1993).

Calligraphic Salutations

Hermann Zapf's letterheadings to Paul Standard

The beginning of a friendship that lasted a lifetime

Privately printed by the Melbert B. Cary, Jr. Graphic Arts Collection

Rochester Institute of Technology · 1993

Paul Standard translated the Typophiles edition of ›Über Alphabete‹ (About Alphabets), and wrote the introduction for ›Pen and Graver‹ in 1952, as well as for ›Typographic Variations‹ (1964). As a calligrapher and teacher, he was very committed to the improvement of handwriting, especially in the direction of Ludovica degli Arrighi's ›Chancery‹.

He passed away at the age of 95 years on January 1, 1992. Our correspondence is stored in the Cary Collection at RIT.

»GEOMETRY

can produce legible letters

Die Geometrie kann lesbare Buchstaben hervorbringen,

but art alone

aber einzig die Kunst

makes them beautiful.

verleiht ihnen Schönheit.

Art begins where geometry ends,

Die Kunst beginnt, wo die Geometrie aufhört,

and imparts to letters

und verleiht den Buchstaben

a character transcending mere

einen Charakter, der nicht mehr meßbar ist.

measurement.«

PAUL STANDARD

›Zapfino Ink‹. Preliminary experiments with the fading effect in letterforms, as if their strokes had been written with liquid ink. These examples were made in 1993 during the Zapfino project. At that time, the intention was to use the fading effect for signatures on documents. Such an effect could add more personality to printed pieces.

The project was ahead of its time. To be prepared for practical use and for technical reasons the alphabet was delayed for several years at Linotype.

20 years earlier, I had reproduced the ink effect in ›Favorite Bible Verses‹, produced by Hallmark Editions, Kansas City 1974. But in 1993, big problems arose trying to get the bleeding effect to work within a tint screen for print. In 2002, the idea came up again after a method to reproduce the effect on a computer had finally been developed.

ST. MATTHEW 6:28
Consider the lilies of the field,
how they grow;
they toil not, neither do they spin.

ST. MATTHEW 6:13
For thine
is
the kingdom,
and
the power,
and the glory,
forever.
AMEN.
1973

List of alphabet designs. Only the most important typefaces I designed between 1938 and 2006 are mentioned; variants such as Italic or Bold are not included. The large letters are set in ›Zapfino‹, while the text lines are set in ›Palatino nova‹.

Key to the abbreviations:
Hallmark = Hallmark Cards, Inc., Kansas City / Missouri. AT&T = American Telephone and Telegraph Company, New York. ITC = International Typeface Corporation, New York. Duensing = Paul H. Duensing, Private Press and Typefoundry, Vicksburg / Michigan. Hell = Dr. Ing. Rudolf Hell, GmbH, Kiel. AMS = American Mathematical Society, Providence / Rhode Island. Scangraphic = Scangraphic Dr. Böger GmbH, Hamburg. URW = Unternehmensberatung Rubow Weber, Hamburg.

…xyz

Alphabets designed by Hermann Zapf from 1938 to 2006.

A — Aldus Book – Al-ahram Arabic – Arno (Hallmark) – Attika Greek – Artemis Greek – Alkor Notation – Aurelia (Hell) – AT&T Garamond

B — Book (ITC New York) – Brush Borders

C — Comenius – Crown Roman (Hallmark) – Chancery (ITC) – Civilité (Duensing) – Charlemagne (Hallmark)

D — Digiset Vario (Hell)

E — Edison (Hell) – Edison Cyrillic – Euler (American Mathematical Society) – Essentials

F — Festival Figures – Firenze (Hallmark) – Frederika Greek

G — Gilgengart Fraktur (1938)

H — Heraklit Greek – Hunt Roman (Pittsburgh)

I — (ITC) International

J — Janson (Linotype) – Jeannette Script (Hallmark)

K — Kompakt Roman

L — Linotype Mergenthaler

M — Melior – Michelangelo Titling – Marconi (Hell) – Musica Notation (C.E. Röder, Leipzig) – Magnus Sans-serif – Medici Script – Missouri (Hallmark)

O — Optima nova – Optima Greek – Orion

N — Novalis – Noris Script

P — Palatino nova – Phidias Greek – Palatino Sans – Palatino Sans Informal – Palatino Arabic – Palatino Greek – Palatino Cyrillic – Primavera Ornaments – Pan Nigerian

Q — Quartz (Xerox Corporation Rochester/New York)

R — Renaissance Antiqua (Scangraphic)

S — Sistina – Sequoya (Cherokee redesign) – Scriptura & Stratford (Hallmark)

T — Trajanus Cyrillic – Textura (Hallmark)

U — Uncial (Hallmark) – URW Sans

V — Vario (Digiset) – Virtuosa – Venture (Linofilm)

W — Winchester (Hallmark) – World Book Modern

X & Y — (For X & Y no inspirations)

Z — Zodiac Signs – Zapfino Extra – Zapfino Ink – Zapf Dingbats (ITC)

›William Morris. Sein Leben und Werk in der Geschichte der Buch- und Schriftkunst‹.
Klaus Blanckertz Publisher, Scharbeutz / Lübeck, 1949.

›Feder und Stichel. Alphabete und Schriftblätter in zeitgemäßer Darstellung.
Geschrieben von Hermann Zapf. In Metall geschnitten von August Rosenberger, Frankfurt‹.
Special edition on Japanese paper: D. Stempel AG, Frankfurt, 1949.
Fabriano mouldmade paper edition: D. Stempel AG, 1950. Trajanus Presse, 1952.

›Pen and Graver. Alphabets and pages of calligraphy by Hermann Zapf, cut in metal
by August Rosenberger‹. Museum Books Inc., New York, 1952.

›Manuale Typographicum. 100 Tafeln in 16 Sprachen gesetzt aus Schriften der D. Stempel AG
unter Verwendung einiger historischer Schriften aus deren Archiv‹. Frankfurt, 1954.
English edition: Museum Books Inc., New York, 1954.
Revised edition: The M.I.T. Press, Cambridge / Mass. and London, 1970.

›Über Alphabete. Gedanken und Anmerkungen beim Schriftentwerfen‹
by Hermann Zapf, D. Stempel AG, Frankfurt, 1960.
›About Alphabets. Some marginal notes on type design‹. The Typophiles, New York, 1960.
(Revised edition): The M.I.T. Press, Cambridge / Mass. and London, 1970.

›Das Blumen-ABC von Hermann Zapf und August Rosenberger‹.
Printing office of D. Stempel AG, Frankfurt, 1948.
Hermann Emig Publisher, Amorbach, 1962.

›Typographische Variationen. 78 Buchtitel und Textseiten als Gestaltungsmöglichkeiten
der Typographie und Buchgraphik‹. G. K. Schauer Publisher, Frankfurt, 1963.
English edition: ›Typographic Variations‹. Museum Books Inc., New York, 1964.
French edition: ›Variations typographiques‹. Hermann (Pierre Berès), Paris, 1965.

›Manuale Typographicum. 100 typographische Gestaltungen über die Schrift, über Typographie
und Druckkunst aus Vergangenheit und Gegenwart‹. (In 18 languages). Z-Presse, Frankfurt, 1968.
English edition: Museum Books Inc., New York, 1968.

›Orbis Typographicus. Thoughts, words and phrases on the arts and sciences.
Experimental typography by Philip Metzger‹. The Crabgrass Press, Prairie Village / Kansas, 1980.

›Hermann Zapf. Hora fugit – Carpe diem. Ein Arbeitsbericht‹.
Technische Hochschule Darmstadt. Maximilian-Gesellschaft, Hamburg, 1984.

›Kreatives Schreiben. Anleitungen und Alphabete‹. Rotring Werke Riepe KG. 1985.
Creative Calligraphy (Engl.). Calligraphies creatives (French). Calligrafia creadora (Spanish edition) 1985.

›Hermann Zapf and his design philosophy. Selected articles and lectures on calligraphy and
contemporary developments in type design‹. Society of Typographic Arts, Chicago / Illinois.
Yale University Press, New Haven / Connecticut, 1987.

›L'opera di Hermann Zapf. Dalla calligrafia alla fotocompositione‹. Edizione Valdonega, Verona, 1991.

›ABC–XYZapf. Fifty years in alphabet design. Professional contributions selected for Hermann Zapf‹. The Wynkyn de Worde Society, London, 1989. Bund Deutscher Buchkünstler, Offenbach, 1989.

›Calligraphic Salutations. Hermann Zapf's letterheadings to Paul Standard‹. Melbert B. Cary, Jr. Graphic Arts Collection, Rochester Institute of Technology, Rochester/New York, 1993.

›Poetry through typography by Hermann Zapf. Poems selected by Walter Schmiele and Peter Frank. Printed in memory of Phil Metzger (1914–1981)‹. Kelly Winterton Press, New York, 1993.

›From the hand of Hermann Zapf. A collection of calligraphy, alphabet design and book typography‹. The Washington Calligraphers Guild, Washington D. C., 1993.

›The design philosophy by Hermann Zapf‹. (English and Japanese). Preface by Carl Zahn. Robundo Publishing Inc. (Jiro Katashio), Tokyo, 1995.

›August Rosenberger 1893–1980. A tribute to one of the great masters of punchcutting, an art now all but extinct‹. Melbert B. Cary, Jr. Graphic Arts Collection, Rochester Institute of Technology, 1966.

›The fine art of letters. The work of Hermann Zapf‹. The Grolier Club, New York, 2000.

›Calligraphic type design in the digital age‹. Friends of Calligraphy Inc., San Francisco. Edited by John Prestianni. Gingko Press, Corte Madera/California, 2001.

›The world of alphabets by Hermann Zapf. A kaleidoscope of drawings and letterforms‹ (CD-ROM). Herzog August Bibliothek Wolfenbüttel. Melbert B. Cary, Jr. Graphic Arts Collection, Rochester Institue of Technology, Rochester/New York, 2001.

›Zapf Essentials. 372 Signs‹. Communication – Office – Markers – Ornaments. (Dingbats redesigns). Type specimen: Linotype GmbH, Bad Homburg, 2002.

›Optima nova with Optima nova Titling‹. Type specimen: Linotype GmbH, Bad Homburg, 2002.

›Zapfino Extra. A Script typeface by Hermann Zapf‹. 4 alphabets for interchangeable use, with many additional characters, newly designed Small Caps, 100 ornaments, and hyper-flourishes. Type specimen: Linotype GmbH, Bad Homburg, 2003.

›Histórias de Alfabetos. A autobiografia e a tipografia de Hermann Zapf‹. Tradução Pedro Maria Soares. Edições Rosari & tupigrafia. São Paulo/Brazil, 2005.

›Palatino nova‹. A classical typeface redesigned with Aldus nova Book, Palatino Titling, Palatino Imperial, Palatino Greek & Palatino Cyrillic. – ›Palatino Arabic‹. 2 type specimens: Linotype GmbH, 2006.

›Palatino Sans. A Supplement to Palatino nova‹. Type specimen: Linotype GmbH, 2006.

›Gudrun Zapf von Hesse. Bucheinbände · Handgeschriebene Bücher · Druckschriften · Schriftanwendungen und Zeichnungen‹. Gesellschaft zur Förderung der Druckkunst. Leipzig, 2002. English edition: Mark Batty, Publisher, West New York/New Jersey, 2002.

Postscript by David Pankow

The RIT Cary Graphic Press is honored to be the co-publisher of this wonderful new book by Hermann Zapf of reminiscences and stories about his typefaces. Are there any other designers of the last 100 years who have exerted such a profound influence on type design and modern typography? Or who have so enthusiastically explored such a variety of technologies for creating type? Or who have brought such endless curiosity and humanity to the world of books and their cultural significance? If so, they would be members of a rare group indeed!

Hermann Zapf's relationship with RIT has been long and productive. Though his active teaching career spanned only a decade, his strong interest in RIT's programs and resources began well before his appointment to the Cary Professorship in 1977, and continues to this day. He speaks generously of the university in the pages of this book, but modestly refrains from taking any credit for the influence he came to exert on those who studied with him. His classes included students from the School of Printing, but also, and more significantly, those classes came to attract an extraordinary group of calligraphers, type designers, and book designers from all over the world. His two-week summer calligraphy sessions, along with the collegial dinners and parties that followed each day's session, became legendary experiences for those who found their way to western New York. No teacher could have been more selfless with his time.

During his tenure as Cary Professor, Hermann Zapf made extensive use of the Cary Graphic Arts Collection, a rare book library devoted to the history of the book and printing, that had been established at RIT in 1969. Its first curator was Alexander S. Lawson, a professor in the School of Printing and a noted authority on type history; under his direction, the Cary Collection developed into an important resource for the students of the School, an intimate place where type specimens and landmark examples of historic printing were readily at hand for class visits. Hermann came to know the collection well and taught his students the importance of examining original manuscripts and early books. Far from praising his own incredible skills as a calligrapher, he pointed with awe to the pages of writing in a thirteenth-century Bible or to the decoration in a fifteenth-century Book of Hours and declared that their anonymous scribes and rubricators were the true craftsmen, individuals whose finely tuned skills with quill pen and simple inks were the envy of modern practitioners of the calligraphic art.

Likewise, Hermann made his students look at the early typefaces of Jenson, Aldus, Arrighi, and Garamond. He spoke intimately of Caslon, Baskerville, and Bodoni, as well as of Morris, Johnston, Goudy, Koch, Trump, and countless other designers, whose work he had studied until the subtle forms and proportions of their types and letterforms were revealed to him. He spoke of his own types as well, fascinating his classes with their histories and antecedents; he showed how some were rooted in classic inscriptions, while others took their inspiration from lettering and calligraphic exercises he had saved since youth. This was teaching at its best: intimate and attentive, master and students engaged in the landscape of learning, where nature, history, and even evolving technologies provided inspiration.

One day, two students came to Hermann with a request. Six months earlier, they had signed up for a special credit project in a papermaking course and were determined to make a sheet of parchment. It was an undertaking that came to consume their days and sorely tested their resolve (as well as that of their classmates). For weeks on end, they attended to a reeking vat of caustic lye in which a sheepskin slowly disgorged its hair on one side and bits of fat and flesh on the other. Once out of the vat, the skin was stretched and scraped, dried and rubbed with pumice until the surface came to resemble – if only distantly – a piece of parchment, the finest of all bookmaking substrates. Would the distinguished Professor Zapf kindly ›write something calligraphic‹ on their skin? Anyone else might have turned them away, unwilling to risk failure in an attempt to ›write something calligraphic‹ on a material that was as stiff as a board, and had the contours of the Appalachian mountain range. But with risk comes learning, and Professor Zapf decided to oblige the trembling students. That piece of parchment still survives, and is today one of the treasures of the Cary Collection: on its wavy surface sits a perfect calligraphic alphabet of such delicacy and beauty that it takes the breath away. In one corner is the signature of Hermann Zapf; in another, ›RIT, 1986‹.

On another occasion, Hermann learned that the ›Specimen-Album‹ of Charles Derriey was available, and urged that it be purchased for the Cary Collection. Published in Paris in 1862, this extravagantly produced volume of decorative types, borders, and calligraphic flourishes is one of the rarest and most beautiful of all nineteenth-century type specimens. This masterpiece of type, composition, and color printing also had a distinguished provenance, since it had once belonged to the well-known type expert Jackson Burke. Though the book came with an expensive price tag, Hermann insisted that its acquisition was vital, if the Cary Collection aspired to become a great center for type studies and printing. The purchase was made, and today, 30 years later, the Charles Derriey specimen forms one of the cornerstones of a type specimen collection of international reputation.

Over the years, Hermann Zapf has continued to support RIT and the Cary Collection, helping us, for example, to acquire a magnificent collection of books and correspondence assembled by Paul Standard, as well as making generous gifts of material from his own archive. Today, the library houses the best collection of Zapf material in any institution outside of Germany, and includes, among the many other treasures, the layouts and proofs for the two editions of his Manuales. Even now, he is

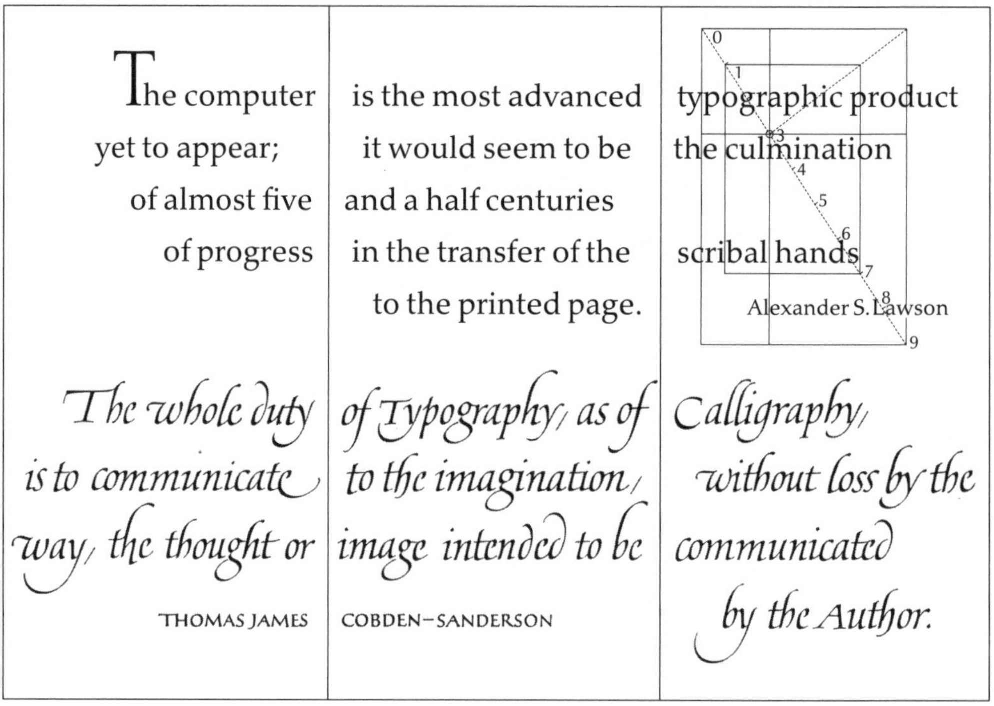
The computer
yet to appear;
of almost five
of progress
is the most advanced
it would seem to be
and a half centuries
in the transfer of the
to the printed page.
typographic product
the culmination
scribal hands
Alexander S. Lawson
The whole duty
is to communicate
way, the thought or
THOMAS JAMES
of Typography, as of
to the imagination,
image intended to be
COBDEN–SANDERSON
Calligraphy,
without loss by the
communicated
by the Author.

in the process of designing a glass wall that will surround a newly constructed facility for the RIT Cary Graphic Arts Press. Formed of 27 eight-foot-high transparent glass panels, the wall will have a series of striking images related to the geometry of book design sandblasted onto its surface, along with some 30 carefully selected quotations from prominent authors and designers about the alphabet, books, reading, and typography, each in a different typeface. Named in honor of Hermann's good friend Alex Lawson, the new facility will declare through its very structure and decoration the fundamental principles of good book design, and will serve as an inspiration for the books that will be conceived and planned within.

The chronicle of Hermann Zapf's life and work has been documented in many publications, including this one. Impressive honors have been bestowed on him, and he is a typographic citizen of many countries. He received, for example, the Frederic W. Goudy Award from RIT, Rochester, 1969; the Johannes Gutenberg Prize, Mainz, 1974; a Gold Medal from the Museo Bodoniano, Parma, 1975; the Euro Design Award, Oostende, 1994, and the Wadim Lazursky Award from the Academy of Graphic Arts, Moscow, 1996. He was designated an Honorary Royal Designer for Industry, London, 1985, and received an honorary doctorate from the University of Illinois. He is an honorary member of numerous prestigious organizations, including the Type Directors Club, New York; the Double Crown Club, London; the Wynkyn de Worde Society, London; the Society of Scribes and Illuminators, London; the Society of Printers, Boston; the Alpha Beta Club, Hong Kong; the Friends of Calligraphy, San Francisco; the Washington Calligraphers Guild, Washington D.C.; the Society of Graphic Designers, Toronto; the Alcuin Society, Vancouver; and many more. He keeps a very busy diary!

When all is said and done, Hermann's story is most indelibly recorded in his calligraphy, his typography, and in all his typefaces. It is in the friendships he has made, the people far and wide that he has inspired, and in the example that he has set. However much new technologies of communication challenge our paradigms of the book and however many new trends come and go, Hermann Zapf has mastered his discipline so purely and so elegantly that his works will remain beautiful and fresh forever.

David Pankow, Curator
Cary Graphic Arts Collection

* A design proposal for 3 of the 27 glass panels surrounding RIT's Lawson Publishing Center. Note the use of both typography and calligraphy for the texts.

This special edition,

including an original typographic print,

was designed by Hermann Zapf

and produced for RIT Cary Graphic Arts Press.

800 copies have been printed.

Typefaces: ›Palatino nova‹ and ›Palatino Sans‹

from www.linotype.com